HELP!
There's a **VEGAN** Coming For Dinner!

Karen Jennings

Published by Art and Soul Interiors
Edited by Alex Jennings
2nd Edition published 2015

ISBN: 978-0-9920826-0-4 (Printed Edition)

Acknowledgements

First, a heartfelt thanks to my mom for showing me that cooking is so much more than overcooked carrots, lumpy mashed potato and a dried up roast, and for letting me experiment in her kitchen. She might have forgotten the day I made an improvised Chinese soup with half a cup of grated fresh ginger, but I haven't!

A huge thank you to my taste-testing teams who were willing to turn up and eat an overwhelming number of dishes per visit. You did a fabulous job, folks!

- Danger Zoners Jody and Po (Dave)
- Ex-pats Sue and Ian, who reminded me about pot pies
- My fabulous friend Margaret and her hubbie Lorne, who look at my food a bit suspiciously but eat it anyway
- The Dinner Club: Brett, Justin, Maggie and Roxane
- The Home Depot Team: Arturo, Carol, Kim, Maggie, Natasha and Victoria
- Kemptville couple: Diane and Warren

And, of course, a huge thank you to my long-suffering family Alan, Alex and Chris, who only occasionally say "Oh dear - can we go out for dinner instead?"

I would also like to thank Tonya, who gave me the push I needed to actually start writing, and my editor, Alex Jennings, who had a few things to say about my typing, spelling, grammar and run-on sentences.

This book is dedicated to the many friends who have said they would love to have me round for dinner, but can't because they wouldn't know what to cook. Without you this book would never have been written.

Contents

Introduction

My eldest son told me a joke recently, which made me smile because it's just so true. Question: How can you tell if someone is a vegan? Answer: You don't have to - they'll tell you. Well, let me tell you... I first started eating a vegetarian (not vegan) diet back in the 80's for the most ignoble of reasons. I couldn't stand the smell of raw meat. At the time, there were no environmental or political or religious motivations, just an offended nose. Admittedly I wore hippy skirts, really liked tofu, wore long dangly earrings, and looked like a stereotypical tree-hugger. I was eating quinoa before most of the western world even knew the word, and despite the lack of evidence I'm still convinced that when I arrived in Canada in the early 90's I got here before tofu did. Over the years I ate the occasional chicken wing (with a dose of Pepto Bismol to help with the resulting indigestion) but have now dropped all meat, egg and dairy products from my diet, partly for ethical reasons and partly because they really don't agree with me. After the last encounter with a milky soup, even my cats wouldn't sleep with me. It was all quite unpleasant.

As the main cook in a household containing a tree nut allergy (the epipen is on stand-by), gluten intolerance (this latest addition has made life interesting!), egg intolerance (nobody enjoys projectile vomiting), two people with lactose intolerance (oh - the gas!!!), three dedicated meat-eaters and a vegan (that's me) I've learned that one diet doesn't fit all. This isn't a book telling you what to eat, but it provides vegans and non-vegans alike with healthy, tasty choices for dinner.

I originally started putting recipes together after leaving my job as a kitchen designer. I realized the need for recipes that my family and friends can actually cook for ME when I visit. No-fuss plant-based meals with no dairy or eggs, which don't require juicing or dehydrating or soaking chia seeds or searching for sea vegetables or other weird stuff. So, here it is: a user-friendly book of recipes for when you want to say "HELP! There's a VEGAN coming for dinner!" By the way, I think I'm free on Saturday...

Karen Jennings

What IS a Vegan Anyway?

There are three main plant-based diets: **Vegetarians** do not eat meat but may eat eggs, milk, cheese and honey. **Vegans** avoid *all* animal-source foods, including dairy and honey and, in some instances, anything which has been refined using animal by-products. A **raw food** diet is usually a vegan diet with the added restriction that the foods must be uncooked and unprocessed. Raw food dieters spend a lot of time in the kitchen peeling, chopping, blending, dehydrating, rehydrating and juicing. The recipes in this book are suitable for vegetarians and vegans, but most are not appropriate for people on a raw food diet.

There are people who simply eat a vegan diet for health reasons, others who eat a vegan diet out of compassion for animals and the environment, while others live the complete vegan lifestyle including avoidance of animal products such as leather and wool. If you are interested in finding out more about eating a healthy plant-based diet, animal rights or factory farming there are some good movies such as Vegucated, Forks over Knives and Food Inc. There are also some useful websites including **www.peta.org** (People for the Ethical Treatment of Animals) – but be warned. PETA can be a bit aggressive in its approach. Also have a look for vegan support groups in your area.

If you are thinking about adopting a vegan diet, there are some excellent websites to help get you started. The Vegan Society (**www.vegansociety.com**) has a lot of tips and recipes. Don't simply stop eating meat, dairy and eggs assuming you will have a balanced diet. As a vegan you need to think about what you are eating to make sure you get adequate amounts of B12, omega 3, iodine and vitamin D. Check out the Vegetarian Resource Group for dietary advice at **http://www.vrg.org/nutrition.**

The term "vegan" was first used by Donald Watson in 1944 and was defined as follows:

Veganism is a way of living which excludes all forms of exploitation of, and cruelty to, the animal kingdom, and includes a reverence for life. It applies to the practice of living on the products of the plant kingdom to the exclusion of flesh, fish, fowl, eggs, honey, animal milk and its derivatives, and encourages the use of alternatives for all commodities derived wholly or in part from animals.

What NOT to Feed to a Vegan

This doesn't claim to be a complete list of foods which contain animal products, but it's a good place to start. Whatever food products you buy ALWAYS read the ingredients when shopping for a vegan meal. The words "pure", "natural" and "organic" are not the same as "vegan".

- Avoid all animal proteins - beef, lamb, chicken, turkey, elk, venison, emu, ostrich... you get the idea.
- Don't serve food containing animal-derived additives such as casein (sometimes found in soy cheeses) and rennet.
- Check your boxed cake mixes – these may contain beef fat.
- Dairy products are not part of a vegan diet, including cream, milk, cheese, whey, butter, some margarines.
- Eggs - vegetarians may eat eggs, vegans don't.
- Fish and seafood are not eaten by vegans - including anchovies.
- Honey might be OK with some dietary vegans, but don't use it if you have any doubts.
- Marshmallows and other gelatin products are made from animals – although you might be able to find vegan marshmallows if you look hard enough.
- Pure food glaze / confectioners glaze is often made from beetle excretions. Yummy, eh?
- Quorn (not currently available in Canada) usually contains egg, although egg-free products may be available in the near future.
- Red candies and cupcake sprinkles may contain dye derived from beetles.
- Refined sugar - there is some debate about whether or not this can be included in a vegan diet. Refined white sugar is passed through a charcoal filter, which sometimes contains animal bone. Brown sugar is usually refined white sugar with the addition of molasses. At the time of writing "Redpath" white sugar is vegan. I buy unrefined raw sugar, which is vegan and tastes really good.
- Some beers and wines are purified using fish bladders - check for vegan friendly options on-line or at your local liquor store, or ask your vegan guest what they like to drink. Better still – ask them to bring a bottle or two when they visit.
- Some flavoured chips and crackers contain powdered cheese or chicken fat.
- The Omega-3 in some enriched products comes from fish. Flax seed omega 3 is fine.
- Worcestershire sauce contains anchovies – look for vegan versions.

Cooking for a Vegan in a Non-Vegan House

There are a few things worth considering when you are having a dinner guest with different dietary habits than your own, regardless of whether they are gluten-free, lactose intolerant, have allergies, or eat a plant-based diet. No-one likes to feel like the odd one out, and definitely don't like being publicly interrogated about their eating habits.

If you're cooking for a mixed group of meat-eaters and vegans, it's worth considering serving everyone a vegan meal. It can be tasty, easy to make and inexpensive, and a reminder that you don't actually *have* to eat meat every day. If you choose to cook a selection of vegan dishes and serve a meat item as a side dish remember to keep the vegan and non-vegan foods separate. Don't use the same cooking or serving utensils for meat and non-meat dishes. And don't feel you have to declare "This dish is vegan, and I made it especially for you" every time something is brought to the table. It can make people feel very awkward and uncomfortable. Trust me on this one! I'm always grateful to the friends who happily throw a veggie burger over the flame pit and treat me like a normal person. No comments of "I bet that tastes like cardboard" or "How can you eat that stuff?" or "Mine's cow. Mmmmmmmmmm." You know who you are. Thank you.

If you're having a lot of guests, consider serving food buffet style or doing a pot luck, but make sure that there are enough non-meat items to keep your vegan visitors fed when the meat eaters start gobbling down the non-meat dishes! Labels are great help for people who have dietary restrictions, including allergies, intolerances and meat-avoidance.

While on a trip to Toronto, Alan and I dropped into a small Chinese restaurant for lunch. I was delighted because the menu had a number of vegetarian items on it. I ordered Tofu with Shanghai Vegetables and checked with the waiter that it didn't contain meat. "No meat?" I asked. "No, no meat. Tofu." he replied. "So NO meat?" I double checked. "NO. No meat. Tofu. Vegetables." Great! When lunch arrived it looked wonderful - tofu with thinly sliced vegetables and deeply browned thin onion strips. I hungrily popped a portion in my mouth and chewed, but there was something very odd going on. The crispy onions were actually small dried fish complete with heads and eyes. Awwww - yuk! There was definitely something a bit fishy about the tofu dish!

A Few Words About The Recipes

I've tried to keep things as simple as possible - no soaking of chia seeds, no juicing, and no hard-to-find ingredients. I purchased all my ingredients from my local supermarket, unless I've specifically mentioned a different source in the recipe. Life's too short to frequently have to go on a hunt for exotic products, although it can be fun for a special occasion.

- I've made each recipe to serve **four people**, based on the assumption that main dishes will be accompanied by rice, potatoes, pasta, bread or another carbohydrate. If you are cooking for very hungry people, feel free to add more beans, faux meat or lentils to a dish.
- I've used 1 tsp of **salt** to season most recipes. This seems to keep most of my diners happy, but I personally like things saltier. Feel free to add more according to your personal tastes. Likewise with **chillies** - I personally like my food HOT but I've reduced the amount of chillies in the recipes to socially acceptable levels.
- Don't feel you have to follow the recipes exactly. Cooking is more of an art than a science and you are free to be creative. If a recipe uses beans but you would rather use faux chicken, go ahead. If you want more garlic, toss it in. If you prefer cabbage over kale, substitute. Do you prefer to use fresh tomatoes instead of canned ones? Go ahead and use them. 4 medium tomatoes are about the same as a **28 oz** can.
- **Fresh herbs** can be used instead of dried ones if you have them, and visa versa. 1 tsp dried is about the same as 1 tbsp fresh.
- When cooking something in the **oven**, remember that not all ovens are the same. Some cook at slightly higher temperatures than the setting while others cook a bit cooler. My poor oven tries its best but is unpredictable even on a good day.
- I use **Kikkoman** brand **soy sauce**, which is widely available. They make a gluten-free variety for those who need it.
- I buy **unrefined raw sugar** because I like the taste more than regular white sugar. The brand I buy is fair trade, which is an added bonus.
- I use **McCormick's "chicken" or "beef" flavour stock cubes**. They're vegan, gluten-free and contain no MSG.

Soups, Salsas and Dips

Appetizers are a great way to keep your guests out from under your feet while you put the finishing touches to dinner. When visitors ask me what they can do to help, I find they respond much better to "You can help me by trying the dip and letting me know what you think" than they do to "Get out of my way if you don't want a pan of hot water accidentally landing on your foot!" Ah, the joys of entertaining.

Salsa and chips or pita and dips are really easy pre-dinner options and take very little time to prepare. When making **salsas**, make sure you use ripe, tasty tomatoes. If you have a local farmer's market it's probably a good place to get good tomatoes when they're in season.

Tomato salsas are incredibly versatile. Use them as a dip for chips, as a side dish for chillies, or use them as a sauce for cooking beans or tofu and serve on top of pasta. If doing the latter, you might want to add a teaspoon of unrefined sugar to reduce the acidity level a little.

Carrot and Lentil Soup with Herb Scones

This soup is excellent served piping hot with miniature herb scones or ice cold on a hot summer's day, sprinkled with some finely chopped mint and green onions.

Soup:
2 tbsp oil
1 medium onion, finely chopped
2 garlic cloves, crushed
2 medium carrots, scrubbed and thinly sliced
2 celery sticks, scrubbed and thinly sliced
1 cup red lentils, soaked for 30 minutes, washed thoroughly and drained
3 cups vegan "chicken flavour" stock
1 tsp salt
¼ tsp ground black pepper
2 tsp lemon juice
2 tbsp fresh parsley, chopped

Scones:
1 ½ cups flour
3 tsp baking powder
1 tsp salt
¼ tsp ground black pepper
3 tbsp vegan margarine
2 tbsp fresh herbs or 2 tsp dried herbs
½ cup plain soy or other non-dairy milk
1 tbsp olive oil

Makes 14 mini scones

Serves 4

1. **To make the soup**, heat the oil in a large pan and fry the onion, garlic, carrots and celery over a high heat for 5 minutes or until soft but not browned.
2. Add the lentils and stock, bring to the boil, reduce the heat, partially cover and simmer gently for 40 minutes, stirring occasionally.
3. Put the soup into a blender and process until smooth. Return to the pan.
4. Stir in the salt, pepper, lemon juice and parsley. Add more stock if the soup is too thick.
5. **To make the scones**, heat the oven to 425'F / 220'C / Gas Mark 7.
6. Mix together the flour, baking powder, salt and pepper. Add the margarine and use your fingertips to rub it into the flour until it resembles fine breadcrumbs. Mix in the herbs.
7. Make a hole in the middle of the flour and pour in the milk and oil. Mix with a knife to form a soft dough. Add more flour or milk as needed.
8. Tip the dough onto a lightly floured surface and pat into a 1" thick circle. Using a shot glass, cut the dough into small circles and transfer to a baking sheet. Allow to rest for 15 minutes before baking for about 20 minutes or until golden brown. Serve warm.

Coconut and Green Bean Soup

This tasty little soup is quick, easy and a lovely golden yellow colour.

3 tbsp olive oil
1 medium carrot, scrubbed and cut into thin strips
2 garlic cloves, crushed
1 tbsp fresh ginger, grated
2 jalapeno chillies, finely chopped
2 tsp lemon rind, finely grated
1 tsp turmeric
1 tbsp ground coriander
4 green onions, finely chopped
1 cup green beans, trimmed and sliced lengthways
1 can / 2 cups coconut milk
2 cups vegan "chicken flavour" stock
3 tsp soy sauce
1 tsp raw unrefined sugar
2 cups bean sprouts
¼ cup fresh basil, chopped

Serves 4

1. Heat the oil in a medium pan and fry the carrots, garlic, ginger and chillies for 5 minutes over a medium heat, stirring frequently. Add the lemon rind, turmeric and coriander and stir fry for another minute.
2. Add the green onions, green beans, coconut milk, stock cube, soy sauce and sugar. Bring to the boil, reduce the heat, cover and simmer gently for 10 minutes.
3. Stir in the bean sprouts and basil, heat for a minute and serve.

If you want to make a meal of it, add some cubed semi-firm tofu when you add the green beans. Put freshly-cooked rice noodles in the bottom of a large bowl and pour the soup over to serve.

Simple Chinese Dip

300g / 11 oz soft tofu
1 tbsp lime juice
2 tbsp soy sauce
2 tsp fresh mint, chopped
¼ tsp red pepper flakes
¼ tsp ground black pepper
½ tsp Chinese 5-spice powder

Chinese Sesame Dip

300g / 11 oz soft tofu
2 tbsp soy sauce
2 tbsp fresh basil, chopped
1 tbsp sesame oil
1 tbsp toasted sesame seeds
1 tbsp rice vinegar
1 tsp fresh ginger, finely chopped
1 tsp unrefined raw sugar
¼ tsp dried crushed chillies

Thai Peanut Dip

1 tsp sesame oil
1 garlic clove, crushed
½ tsp dried crushed red chillies
½ cup water
½ cup peanut butter, crunchy or smooth
4 tbsp soy sauce
2 tbsp rice vinegar
2 green onions, finely chopped (these go on top, not in the blender)

The instructions for all three dips are the same. Put everything in the blender and process until smooth. Serve with sliced vegetables, or whatever else you would like to dip.

Eggplant Dip

This is a nice addition to a chip-and-dip line-up and is very easy to make. It takes time to roast the eggplant but after that it's really just blender time!

1 large eggplant
6 cloves of garlic
2 tbsp olive oil
1 tsp salt
¼ tsp ground black pepper
2 tbsp tahini
1 tbsp dried parsley
2 tbsp lemon juice
1 small jar artichoke hearts, drained and rinsed

Makes about 1 ½ cups

1. Heat the oven to 400'F / 200'C / Gas Mark 6.
2. Wash and dry the eggplant then make some deep cuts in the top. Peel the garlic cloves and pop them inside the slits. This stops them from drying out while roasting. Bake for 45 minutes - 1 hour or until the eggplant is soft and starts to shrivel.
3. When cool enough to handle, scrape the inside of the eggplant along with the garlic into a blender. Add the olive oil, salt, pepper, tahini, parsley, lemon juice and artichoke hearts. Process until smooth. Taste and add more lemon juice or salt according your preferences. Serve chilled or at room temperature with crackers, bread, chips or veggies.

Guacamole in Mushrooms

Guacamole is often just a simple smooth green paste served with salsa and chips, but it can be much more exciting than that. I personally prefer mine to be a bit chunky rather than sludgy, with chillies or tomatoes or other bits of texture and flavour. Avocado goes brown when exposed to air, so make guacamole as close as possible to serving. If you need to make it ahead of time, pour a thin layer of olive oil on the surface to slow down the oxidization and keep it looking green longer.

2 tbsp onion or green onions, finely chopped
1 jalapeno chilli, finely chopped
¼ tsp salt
¼ cup fresh coriander, finely chopped
1 large avocado
Small splash of lime juice
20 small white or coffee mushrooms, wiped clean and stems removed
Optional Additional Ingredients:
1 tomato, finely chopped
½ cucumber, finely chopped
¼ cup fresh pineapple, finely chopped
1 small garlic clove, finely chopped

Makes about 1 ½ cups

1. Mix the onion, chilli, salt and coriander together. If you want, use a mortar or small blender to squash it all together to form a paste.
2. Scoop out the avocado flesh and add to the onion mixture. Either mash it coarsely with a fork to make a chunky guacamole or turn it into a smooth paste.
3. Stir in any of the optional extra ingredients.
4. Taste and add lime juice and more salt or chilli if you like. Stuff into the mushrooms.

Hummus

This is so easy to make that you may never buy store-made hummus again.

1 can / 2 cups cooked chickpeas, rinsed
¼ cup lemon juice (about 1 large lemon)
¼ cup tahini
1 garlic clove, chopped
2 tbsp olive oil, plus more for serving

1 tsp salt
½ tsp cumin
3 tbsp water
Pinch of paprika for serving

Makes about 1 ½ cups

1. Put the chick peas, lemon juice, tahini, garlic, olive oil, salt, cumin and water in a blender. Process until smooth. Serve drizzled with a little olive oil and sprinkled with paprika.

Hummus with Red Pepper

This sweet dip makes a nice change from standard hummus.

1 red pepper
1 can / 2 cups chickpeas, rinsed
1/3 cup tahini
¼ cup lemon juice

2 tbsp olive oil plus some for serving
2 garlic cloves, chopped
1 tsp salt
Pinch of paprika

Makes about 2 cups

1. Heat the oven to 400'F / 200'C / Gas Mark 6.
2. Wash and dry the pepper then bake for 45 minutes - 1 hour or until soft and charred. Put into a dish and cover with plastic wrap.
3. When cool enough to handle, remove the seeds and peel the charred skin off the pepper. Put the flesh into a blender. Add the tahini, lemon juice, olive oil, garlic and salt. Process until smooth. Taste and add more lemon juice or salt according your preferences.

Mushroom Pate

Use whatever mushrooms you have on hand to make this pate. I usually use a mixture of cremeni (coffee), white and portabella mushrooms. Spread this on crackers or use as a dip. Yes, I know it's a bit of an earthy colour, but it tastes great.

If you want a bit of a kick, fry a chopped jalapeno chilli along with the mushrooms.

2 tbsp olive oil
1 tbsp vegan margarine
1 medium onion, finely chopped
3 garlic cloves, coarsely chopped
About 6 cups sliced mixed mushrooms (400g)
1 tsp salt
Dash of ground black pepper
1 avocado, pitted and chopped
1 tbsp balsamic vinegar

Makes about 1 ½ cups

1. Heat the oil and margarine in a large frying pan and add the onion, garlic, mushrooms, salt and pepper. Fry over a high heat for 10 minutes, stirring occasionally.
2. Transfer the vegetables to a blender and add the avocado and vinegar. Process until it looks the way you like it. Some like it smooth while others like it to have some chunks.
3. Put into little dishes and chill for a couple of hours before serving.

Salsa with Garlic

Oooooh - garlicky! Useful if you're being harassed by a vampire... but not so good if you're planning on being romantic later!

This salsa can actually be made two different ways. The first includes raw garlic, which is quite pungent, while the second option cooks the garlic which mellows it considerably. Either way, it's really nice either on top of chips or used as a topping for chillies or stews.

½ cup red onion, finely chopped
1 jalapeno chilli, deseeded if desired, finely chopped
12 garlic cloves, finely chopped
½ tsp salt
3 red or yellow tomatoes, finely chopped
1 tsp dried basil

Makes 1 - 1 ½ cups

Option 1: Raw Salsa

Mix everything together and leave in the fridge for 20 minutes for the flavours to mingle.

Option 2: Cooked Salsa

1. Put 1 tbsp olive oil in a small pan and fry the onion, chilli and garlic over a medium heat for 5 minutes or until softened.
2. Stir in the salt, tomatoes and basil and continue to cook gently for 10 minutes. Allow to cool before serving.

Tomato Salsa

Yes, I know you can easily pick up a jar of salsa from the grocery store and serve it with tortilla chips, but sometimes it's nice to have a homemade one instead. If you're in the mood to knock something together yourself, there are two options here. The first uses cooked tomatoes out of a can and resembles a store-bought jar of salsa, while the second uses fresh tomatoes. Make sure they are ripe and preferably organic - I find they really do taste better than standard grocery store tomatoes. These home-made salsas obviously contain no hidden ingredients and are ideal for people who wish to avoid additives or artificial products. You can control the level of heat by adding more chillies, and can add more salt or garlic to taste. If you like, you can also add some chopped fresh green pepper.

1 can (28 oz) diced tomatoes, drained OR 3 large, ripe tomatoes, chopped
1 jalapeno chilli, finely chopped
6 green onions, thinly sliced
¼ cup chopped fresh coriander
2 tbsp lime juice
Pinch of ground black pepper
1 garlic clove, finely chopped
¼ tsp salt

Makes about 2 ½ cups

1. Mix together the tomatoes, chilli, onions, coriander, lime juice, black pepper, garlic and salt.
2. Cover and chill at least 4 hours.

Tomato and Pineapple Salsa

This salsa-with-a-twist uses roasted pineapple to give it a sweet and sour flavour. You can make a mild version without the chipotles, or a spicy, smokey one with the chillies. I find cans of chipotle chillies in adobe sauce in the Mexican food isle of my local supermarket, natural food store or speciality Mexican store.

3 medium tomatoes
4 thick slices of pineapple (about ½"
thick)
½ tbsp olive oil
4 green onions, thinly sliced
4 garlic cloves, crushed
½ tsp black pepper
¼ tsp ground allspice
½ cup fresh coriander, chopped
¼ cup orange juice

2 tbsp lime juice
2 tbsp white vinegar
1 ½ tsp sugar
1 ½ tsp salt

Optional Ingredients:
2 chipotle chillies in adobo sauce
1 jalapeno chilli, finely chopped
½ green pepper, finely chopped

Makes about 4 cups
1. Heat the oven to 450'F / 230'C / Gas Mark 8
2. Cover a baking tray with foil. Brush the pineapple rings with oil and cut a cross in the top of the tomatoes. Bake for 40 - 45 minutes or until soft with brown patches.
3. Peel the loose skin off the tomatoes and coarsely chop the flesh.
4. Mix together the tomatoes, pineapple, olive oil, green onions, garlic, pepper, allspice, coriander, orange juice, lime juice, vinegar, sugar and salt.
5. If you are making spicy salsa, add the chipotle chillies, green chilli and green pepper.
6. Allow to sit for 30 minutes, then drain off excess liquid before serving.

Sweet Potato Balls with Mango Dip

You can cook the balls ahead of time and serve at room temperature, or reheat them in a 350'F / 180'C / Gas Mark 4 oven for 20 minutes.

Balls:
2 sweet potatoes
2 tbsp sugar
2 tbsp grated fresh ginger
1 tsp cinnamon
1 tsp allspice
1 tsp crushed dried red chillies
1 tsp salt
1 ¼ cups flour
1 ½ cups sesame seeds
Vegetable oil for deep frying

Dip:
1 ripe mango
2 tsp maple syrup or unrefined raw sugar
¼ tsp ground ginger
¼ tsp crushed dried red chilli
1 tbsp lime or lemon juice

Makes 25 - 30 balls, depending on size

1. Cook the sweet potatoes in the microwave for about 10 minutes, or in the oven at 350'F / 180'C / Gas Mark 4 for about 45 minutes. Allow to cool, then peel and mash. You should have about 2 cups.
2. Stir in the sugar, ginger, cinnamon, allspice, chillies, salt and flour. It should form a firm dough. Add a small amount of extra flour if needed.
3. Shape the dough into small balls and roll in sesame seeds.
4. In a large, deep pan, heat enough oil to cover at least half a ball. Do not fill your pan more than 1/3 full of oil. When the oil is hot fry the balls for about 3 minutes, turning over halfway through, or until golden. Remove and drain off the excess oil. You will probably have to do this in batches.
5. To make the dip, put the mango, maple syrup or sugar, ginger, chilli and lime/lemon juice into a small blender. Blend until smooth.

Beans

Beans have had a bad rap over the years as being the cause of flatulence and other digestive inconveniences due to their fabulously high fibre content, but they're very nutritious and can be delicious. I always use beans out of a can so I don't have to worry about rinsing and soaking and inconveniently long cooking times. If you want to cook your own, go ahead, but my can opener and I will not be separated any time soon.

There are many types of beans available, and for the most part they are interchangeable in a recipe. They have different tastes and textures, and you may find that you like some beans but not others.

- **Black beans** have a velvety texture and a subtly sweet taste. They go well with smoky flavors, chipotle or vegan bacon.

- **Black eyed peas** are small and spotted. They have a nice earthy taste which goes well in spicy stews.

- **Cannellini beans,** also known as **white kidney beans**, have a mild creamy flavour. I like to use them in chillies to give the dish a bit more visual interest than using plain old red kidney beans.

- **Chick peas**, also known as **garbanzo beans**, are round with a nutty flavour. I use them in curries, chillies, stews, couscous dishes and to make hummus.

- **Kidney beans** are red on the outside and creamy white on the inside. They are commonly used in chillies but also make a good curry or stew.

- **Lima beans** are large and white and often mushy. I hate 'em!

- **Pinto beans** are pale with lots of spots. They have an earthy taste and a smooth texture. I like to pop them into pasta sauces.

African Black Eyed Peas

I can't always find cans of black eyed peas in my grocery store, so I use black beans instead. Serve with rice, couscous or quinoa.

1 can / 2 cups cooked black eyed peas, rinsed and drained
¼ cup olive oil (or vegan margarine)
1 medium red onion, finely chopped
1 large tomato, finely chopped
1 jalapeno chili, finely chopped
2 garlic cloves, finely chopped
1 tsp grated fresh ginger
¼ tsp ground fenugreek (methi)
1 tsp cumin
¼ tsp ground cardamom

¼ tsp ground cloves
½ tsp cinnamon
½ tsp allspice
1 tsp turmeric
1 tbsp dried oregano
2 tsp dried basil
1 cup coconut milk
1 cup water or stock
1 tsp salt
2 tbsp chopped coriander leaves

Serves 4

1. Heat the oil in a medium saucepan. Add the onion, tomato and chili. Fry over a medium low heat for about 10 minutes or until the onion is soft.
2. Add the garlic, ginger, fenugreek, cumin, cardamom, cloves, cinnamon, allspice and turmeric. Fry for 30 seconds then add the oregano, basil, coconut milk and stock. Simmer for 20 minutes.
3. Stir in the black eyed peas and salt. Simmer for another 20 minutes. Sprinkle with coriander leaves and serve.

Allspice Black-Eyed Beans with Earl Grey Tea Quinoa

The tea infuses the quinoa with a subtle "earthy" flavour, but if you want a more intense bergamot taste let the tea bags steep for longer.

4 tbsp olive oil
1 medium onion, coarsely chopped
4 garlic cloves, chopped
1 jalapeno chilli, thinly sliced
1 red pepper, finely chopped
2 tsp allspice
½ tsp cinnamon
¼ tsp ground cloves
1 tsp salt
1 tsp ground black pepper
3 large tomatoes, chopped
1 "chicken flavour" vegan stock cube

½ tsp dried thyme
1 tbsp dried oregano
4 tbsp dried parsley
2 cups / 1 can cooked black eyed beans
1 large bunch kale, chopped

Quinoa:
1 ½ cups dried quinoa
3 cups brewed earl grey tea
(Use 2 tea bags and steep for 10 minutes)

Serves 4

1. Heat the oil in a large saucepan. When hot, add the onion, garlic, jalapeno chilli and red pepper. Cook over a medium heat until soft, about 5 minutes.

2. Add the allspice, cinnamon and cloves. Cook for 1 minute or until fragrant.

3. Add the salt, black pepper, tomatoes, stock cube, thyme, oregano and parsley. Reduce the heat to low, cover and simmer for 30 minutes.

4. While the sauce is cooking, prepare the quinoa. I just throw mine in the rice cooker but you can cook it on the stove. Bring the tea to a boil and stir in the quinoa. Stir, cover and simmer over a very low heat for 15 - 20 minutes or until all the water has been absorbed. Set aside, covered, until the beans are ready.

5. Stir the beans and kale into the tomato sauce. Cover and simmer gently for 10 minutes.

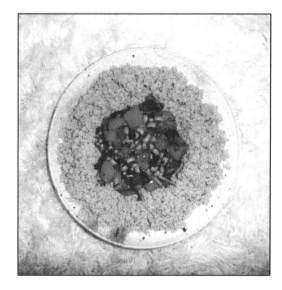

Beans Bourguignon

You can use just about any type of cooked bean for this dish, such as borlotti, pinto, kidney or black beans. I like to serve this topped with hot pepper sauce. But then again, I like most things topped with hot pepper sauce!

2 tbsp olive oil
20 baby onions,
4 carrots, peeled and sliced
5 garlic cloves, finely chopped
30 baby mushrooms
1 tsp dried thyme
1 tsp dried rosemary
1 bay leaf
1 cup diced tomatoes

2 tbsp tomato paste
1 ½ cups vegan stock (I use beef flavour)
1 cup dry red wine
4 cups / 2 cans cooked Romano beans
1 tsp salt
½ tsp ground black pepper
2 tbsp flour mixed with 2 tbsp olive oil.

Serves 4

1. In a large pan, heat the oil and fry the onions, carrots, garlic and mushrooms for 10 minutes over a medium heat.
2. Stir in the thyme, rosemary, bay leaf, tomatoes, tomato paste, stock and wine. Bring to a boil, reduce the heat, cover and simmer gently for 30 minutes or until the vegetables are tender.
3. Rinse and drain the beans. Add to the pan along with the salt, and pepper. Continue to simmer for another 20 minutes.
4. Add the oil and flour mixture to the pan and stir while it thickens. If it gets too thick add a little more wine. Serve with French bread or mashed potatoes.

Black Eyed Pea Curry

One of my pet peeves is when a cookbook author writes things like "many people in India are vegetarian, and there are a large number of meatless recipes" and then proceeds to have nothing but lamb, beef and chicken curries on the following pages. Trust me, there actually are many tasty vegetarian curries, and here is one of them. Serve with rice.

3 tbsp vegetable oil
1 tsp cumin seeds
1 medium onion, coarsely chopped
1 tbsp fresh ginger, grated
3 garlic cloves, coarsely chopped
1 jalapeno chilli, sliced
½ tsp hot cayenne powder
½ tsp turmeric
2 tsp garam masala
4 large tomatoes, coarsely chopped
½ tsp sugar
1 tsp salt
1 can / 2 cups cooked black eyed peas, rinsed and drained

Serves 4

1. Heat the oil in a large frying pan then add the cumin seeds. Fry for 1 minute then add the onion, ginger, garlic and chilli. Fry over a medium heat until the onion is soft, about 5 minutes.
2. Add the cayenne, turmeric and garam masala and continue to cook over a medium heat for 1 minute.
3. Stir in the tomatoes, sugar and salt and cook over a medium heat until the tomatoes are falling apart.
4. Stir in the cooked black eyed peas, cover and simmer over a low heat for about 20 minutes.

Black Beans with Chipotle Chilli and Adobe Sauce

Chipotle chillies in adobe sauce are available in my local grocery store from time to time in the Mexican food section, but can also be purchased from Mexican grocers. Chipotles are smoked jalapeno chillies and adobe sauce is quite smoky. Three chipotle and one tablespoon of sauce is all you need to make this chilli, but add more if you like your food hot. Pop the remains of the can in a freezer bag and freeze for another day.

2 tbsp olive oil
1 large onion, finely chopped
6 garlic cloves, crushed
3 chipotle chillies, finely chopped
1 tbsp adobe sauce from the chipotle can
¼ tsp ground black pepper
1 can (28 oz) diced tomatoes
1 tbsp dried oregano
½ tbsp dried basil
2 cans / 4 cups cooked black beans, rinsed
1 cup chopped fresh parsley

Serves 4

1. Heat the oil in a medium pan and cook the onions and garlic over a medium heat for 5 minutes or until soft.
2. Stir in the chipotle chillies, adobe sauce, pepper, tomatoes, oregano and basil. Bring to the boil then reduce the heat, cover and simmer gently for 30 minutes to let the flavours mingle.
3. Add the black beans and continue to cook for another 10 minutes. Stir in the parsley and serve with rice.

Chickpea and Cabbage Tagine

This dish is very easy to make using canned chick peas and canned tomatoes. Serve with rice, couscous or quinoa.

6 tbsp olive oil
1 medium onion, coarsely chopped
1 garlic clove, coarsely chopped
½ tsp crushed dried red chillies
½ tsp ground coriander
1 tsp caraway seeds
1 tsp paprika
½ tsp ground ginger
½ tsp turmeric
1 ½ tsp cumin

1 tsp cinnamon
1 tsp salt
1 can (28 oz) diced tomatoes
2 tsp unrefined raw sugar
1 can / 2 cups cooked chickpeas, rinsed
2 cups finely shredded white cabbage
¼ cup finely chopped fresh parsley
¼ cup finely chopped fresh coriander

Serves 4

1. Heat the oil in a large saucepan. Add the onion and fry over a medium heat for 5 minutes or until softened.
2. Add the garlic, chillies, ground coriander, caraway seeds, paprika, ground ginger, turmeric, cumin, cinnamon and salt. Fry over a gentle heat for a minute or until fragrant.
3. Add the diced tomatoes, sugar and chickpeas. Cover and simmer for 20 minutes.
4. Add the cabbage, parsley and coriander. Cook for about 5 minutes or until the cabbage is starting to soften. Don't overcook.

Easiest Curry EVER

It doesn't get any easier than this to make a curry! The basic ingredients are all in a packet or a can and you just need to throw it all together. Adjust the quantities according to your personal tastes. I've used black eyed peas here, but you could use chick peas, faux chicken breasts, cubed firm tofu and green peas, cooked lentils, potatoes and cauliflower, or whatever else you have on hand.

2 tbsp vegetable oil
1 onion, finely chopped
4 garlic cloves, finely chopped
1 tbsp fresh ginger, finely chopped
6 - 8 tbsp curry powder, or to taste
2 tbsp water
1 can / 2 cups coconut milk
2 tbsp tomato paste
1 vegan "chicken" flavour stock cube
1 tsp salt (more if needed)
1 can / 2 cups cooked black eyed peas, rinsed
½ cup fresh coriander (optional)

Serves 4 (add an extra can of beans if you're really hungry)

1. Heat the oil in a medium pan and fry the onion, garlic and ginger for 5 minutes or until soft.
2. Add the curry powder and water. Stir over a medium heat for 2 minutes or until fragrant.
3. Mix in the coconut milk, tomato paste, stock cube, salt and black eyed peas. Bring to the boil, reduce the heat, cover and simmer gently for 20 minutes. Add a small amount of water if it gets too thick. Sprinkle with coriander before serving if you have some.

Curry mixes comes in a variety of shapes, sizes and heat intensity. Some of my friends refer to it as "That yellow stuff found in a packet in the spice isle." I cringe when I hear that - I'm a curry snob who usually mixes up her own spice blends - but I know not everyone has the time or inclination to do that.

Chick Pea Cinnamon Couscous

Feel free to adjust the vegetables according to what you have on hand. Try parsnips, carrots or pumpkin, for example.

2 large sweet potatoes (about 4 cups when cubed)
20 baby carrots, or one large sliced carrot
1 large onion, cut into chunks
4 tbsp olive oil
1 tsp ground ginger
2 tsp cinnamon
2 tsp brown sugar
1 tsp salt
½ tsp crushed dried red chilli
4 garlic cloves, crushed
1 can / 2 cups cooked chickpeas, rinsed
¼ cup vegan "chicken flavour" stock

Couscous:
3 cups vegan "chicken flavour" stock
1 tsp olive oil
1 tbsp dried parsley
1 ½ cups dried couscous
¼ cup fresh coriander, chopped

Serves 4

1. Heat the oven to 400'F/ 200'C / Gas Mark 6.
2. Put the sweet potato cubes, carrots and onion in a resealable plastic bag with the olive oil, ginger, cinnamon, sugar, salt, chilli and garlic. Shake until the vegetables are well coated then tip into a baking tray. Cover with foil and bake for 25 minutes.
3. Remove the foil and stir in the chickpeas and stock. Cook uncovered for another 20 minutes or until the sweet potato is soft.
4. When the vegetables are almost ready, bring the extra stock to a boil and stir in the couscous, olive oil and dried parsley. Cover tightly and leave to sit for 10 minutes before fluffing with a fork. Serve topped with the roasted vegetables and coriander.

Chickpea Tuscan Stew

Swiss chard is supposedly one of the healthiest vegetables around, which is fairly useless information if you don't happen to like the taste. It's quite bitter when raw but mellows when cooked. If you really don't like it, use kale and follow the recipe below or use spinach instead, but add it just 5 minutes before serving the stew.

1 large bunch Swiss chard, stalks removed
⅓ cup olive oil
1 medium onion, finely chopped
2 garlic cloves, crushed
½ tsp red chili pepper flakes
1 can / 2 cups cooked chickpeas, rinsed
¼ tsp freshly ground black pepper
3 tbsp tomato paste
¼ cup sliced olives

½ cup boiling water
1 vegan "chicken" flavour stock cube
1 tsp dried basil
½ tsp salt
4 slices toasted French bread (dairy free)
Olive oil for drizzling
½ cup chopped fresh basil, or a mix of fresh basil, oregano and parsley

Serves 4

1. Cut the Swiss chard into wide ribbons, wash and drain.
2. Heat the oil in a large saucepan. Add the onion, garlic and chili flakes. Cook for about 5 minutes or until the onion is soft.
3. Add the chickpeas and stir to coat with the oil. Add the chard, black pepper, tomato paste and olives along with enough water to just cover the ingredients. Stir in the stock cube and basil.
4. Cover and simmer gently over a low heat for 40 minutes. Taste and add salt if needed, depending on how salty the olives were.
5. Arrange a slice of toasted French bread at the bottom of each of 4 bowls. Drizzle with a little olive oil. Put the stew over the toast and sprinkle fresh herbs on top. Serve immediately.

Paprika Bean Pasta

If you like heat, you can make this into a spicy little number with the addition of a chopped green jalapeno or two thrown in with the sweet peppers.

3 tbsp olive oil
1 onion, thinly sliced
1 red pepper, thinly sliced
1 yellow pepper, thinly sliced
3 garlic cloves, crushed
2 sticks of celery, thinly sliced
1 tbsp paprika
1 tsp crushed dried red chilli
½ tsp ground black pepper
1 jar (650 ml) pasta sauce
1 cup fruity white wine or stock
1 can / 2 cups cooked pinto beans, rinsed
½ cup grated vegan "cheese" (optional)
450g / 1 lb small pasta such as orzo

Serves 4

1. Heat the oil in a large frying pan and add the onion, peppers, garlic and celery. Cook over a medium-high heat for 10 minutes or until the onion is soft and golden.
2. Stir in the paprika, chilli and black pepper and cook for 2 minutes. Add the pasta sauce, white wine and beans. Mix well, bring to the boil, cover and simmer on a low heat for 30 minutes.
3. Cook the pasta in a large pan of boiling water for 10 - 12 minutes, drain and stir into the sauce. Serve immediately topped with grated "cheese" if you like that sort of thing.

Soybean Curry

I always use cooked soybeans out of a can, but you can cook your own if you have the time. Dried soybeans must be soaked overnight, and generally take 2 - 3 hours to cook. Check your packet for specific instructions on how to cook the brand you buy. This recipe can also be made using other beans, such as chick peas or black eyed peas.

4 tbsp vegetable oil
1 large onion, finely chopped
4 garlic cloves, crushed
2 tbsp finely chopped fresh ginger
1 or 2 jalapeno chillies, finely chopped
10 curry leaves
1 tsp mustard seeds
½ tsp crushed dried red chillies
1 tsp turmeric

1 tbsp ground coriander
1 cup coconut milk
2 medium tomatoes, chopped
1 can / 2 cups cooked soybeans, rinsed
4 tsp balsamic vinegar
1 tsp salt
1 tsp ground black pepper
Handful chopped fresh coriander

Serves 4

1. Heat the oil in a large frying pan. Add the onion and cook until deep golden brown, about 10 minutes.
2. Reduce the heat and add the garlic, ginger, jalapeno chillies and curry leaves. Fry for 2 minutes then add the mustard seeds. Fry until they begin to crackle (watch out - they can jump out of the pan). Add the dried chilli, turmeric and coriander and mix well.
3. Stir in the coconut milk, tomatoes and soybeans. Bring to the boil then reduce the heat, cover and simmer for 10 minutes or longer to let the flavours develop.
4. Stir in the vinegar and cook for 2 more minutes. Add the salt and pepper and serve topped with fresh coriander.

A Few Words About Coconut Milk

Thick / Premium Coconut Milk

This has the highest fat content of the canned varieties. The brand I buy has about 12g of fat in 60ml. It's the best choice when you need a rich taste, such as in desserts and sweet sauces, but it's also good in both Indian and Thai curries. You can also open the can from the bottom and drain off the liquid, then use the remaining solids to make a delicious dessert topping by folding in 2 tbsp powdered sugar.

It does have a high fat content and a lot of calories. It's nice to use when having someone over for dinner, but it's probably best not to eat it too often if you're watching your weight.

Regular coconut

This has less fat (about 5g fat per 60 ml) than the premium variety and works well in curries and soups. This is the coconut milk I use most often. Shake the can well if you are planning on only using half of it to mix the coconut cream back into the coconut water as they usually separate out over time.

Lite coconut milk

This is probably OK for shakes and smoothies, but I never buy it so I don't really know!

Creamed coconut

This solid block of coconut cream is a handy thing to have around in case you run out of canned coconut milk. It's also useful if you want to make a thick curry sauce - cut off a thick slice and toss it into the curry instead of using coconut milk and add water as needed.

Coconut Milk for Drinking

Coconut milk is available for pouring on your cereals and can be found next to soy milk and almond milk products. Don't use this one in curries - it's much too thin.

Lentils

There are many types of lentils to choose from, including red, green, brown, puy, urad, masoor, mung, tuvar and yellow. They are all high in fibre and nutrients.

I use a wide variety of lentils when making Indian meals, but in this book I've stuck mostly to **split red lentils**, which are easy to find and simple to cook. Strictly speaking, red lentils don't need soaking, but I usually leave them sitting in water for 30 minutes because I find it reduces the amount of foaming when they are boiling. It's very important to wash lentils well before cooking them and pick out any small stones which may have made their way into the bag. It's not nice when you or a guest accidentally chip a tooth on a piece of rock hidden in a plate of lentils.

Red lentils are a great substitute for ground meat in chillies, curries and pies. They take 20 - 30 minutes to cook, depending on how old they are. Don't add salt to the cooking water, as it seems to stop them from cooking properly. Also, remember to only partially cover the pan when cooking lentils - they have tendency to boil over if fully covered, which can be a bit of a pain to clean up.

I also like **split urad dhal**, which are small, white and skinless. They are quick to cook and easy to digest, with a mild, creamy taste. I buy my urad dhal from the Indian grocery store, although my local supermarket occasionally also has them. I occasionally cook **green lentils, brown lentils** and **yellow split peas** from scratch, but I find it much easier to just open a can and rinse them well. Green and brown lentils are good in herbed soups and stews or in lasagne or pies, while yellow split peas go well with spices.

Easy Lentil Spaghetti Bolognaise

Is there anyone who doesn't like a tomato sauce on top of pasta? If you want it *very* tomatoey, stir in 2 tbsp of tomato paste along with the pasta sauce.

1 cup red lentils, soaked for 30 minutes in cold water then washed and drained
1 ½ cups water
1 onion, finely chopped
3 garlic cloves, crushed
2 bay leaves
1 jar pasta sauce
1 vegan stock cube
½ tbsp balsamic vinegar
1 tbsp dried oregano
2 tsp dried basil
2 tsp salt
½ tsp ground black pepper
450g pasta

Serves 4

1. Put the washed, drained lentils in a medium size pan with the water, onion, garlic and bay leaves. Bring to the boil and carefully skim off any foam which develops. Reduce the heat, mostly cover with a lid and simmer gently for 20 minutes or until soft, checking from time to time that the mixture is not burning on the bottom of the pan. Add a small amount of water if needed.
2. When the lentils are soft, stir in the pasta sauce, stock cube, balsamic vinegar, oregano, basil, salt and black pepper. Cover and simmer gently for 15 minutes.
3. Serve with pasta.

Lentil Potato Hotpot

This curry powder in this hotpot is very subtle, but if you don't like things to be spicy leave it out and add 1 tbsp dried oregano and 2 tsp dried basil instead.

1 can / 2 cups cooked green lentils, rinsed
5 medium potatoes
3 tbsp vegetable oil
1 large onion, chopped
2 medium carrots, sliced
3 celery sticks, sliced
4 garlic cloves, crushed

1 - 2 tbsp curry powder
1 can (28 oz) diced tomatoes
1 vegan chicken flavour stock cube
2 tbsp tomato paste
1 tsp salt
½ tsp ground black pepper
2 tbsp dried parsley

Serves 4

1. Heat the oven to 400'F/ 200'C / Gas Mark 6
2. Put the potatoes in a large pan of water and boil for 20 minutes or until tender. Drain.
3. In a large frying pan, heat the oil and fry the onion, carrots, celery and garlic over a medium heat for 10 minutes, or until the onions are soft. Add the curry powder and fry for another 2 minutes.
4. Add the tomatoes, stock cube, tomato paste, salt, pepper and parsley. Bring to the boil then reduce the heat, cover and simmer gently for 10 minutes.
5. Stir in the lentils and transfer the mixture to a 9" x 13" oven proof dish.
6. Chop the potatoes into small pieces (or carefully slice into circles if you prefer) and place on top of the lentils.
7. Put the dish on a tray to catch drips and bake for 45 minutes or until bubbling and lightly browned.

Red Lentils with Garlic (Tarka Dhal)

This curry is about as simple as you can get. No fancy techniques, lightly spiced and really delicious. Serve with rice for a complete dinner or halve the quantities and serve as a side dish with a vegetable curry.

2 cups red lentils
1 onion, finely chopped
4 cups water
½ tsp turmeric
½ tsp ground ginger
½ tsp cumin
1 bay leaf

Final Fry:
6 tbsp oil
6 garlic cloves, thinly sliced
8 curry leaves
1 tsp salt
2 tbsp coriander leaves, finely chopped

Serves 4

1. Wash the lentils multiple times and then soak them in cold water for 30 minutes. Strictly speaking, red lentils don't usually need soaking - check your packet for instructions on how to prepare and cook the brand you buy - but I do it anyway.
2. Put the lentils and onion in a large pan with 4 cups of water. Stir in the turmeric, ginger, cumin and bay leaf. Bring to the boil then reduce the heat and simmer, partially covered, for about 30 minutes or until the lentils are tender. If foam forms on top of the lentils, carefully skim it off and throw it away.

3. For the final fry, heat the oil in a small frying pan. When hot, add the garlic and cook until golden brown - about 3 minutes. Add the curry leaves and salt and cook for another 30 seconds. Pour the oil over the lentils - it should be hot enough to spit.
4. Serve sprinkled with fresh coriander leaves.

Red Lentils with Coconut Milk

Coconut milk gives a nice creamy taste to these spiced lentils, which can be served as a vegetarian dinner with rice or bread and some pickles, or as part of a larger Indian dinner. Make half the quantity if you are using it as a side dish.

4 cups water
2 cup red lentils
2 cloves organic garlic, finely chopped
2 tsp fresh ginger, grated.
1 medium onion, finely chopped
1 green pepper, thinly sliced (optional)
2 tsp cayenne powder

1 tsp turmeric
1 tsp garam masala
1 tsp ground cardamom
1 tsp unrefined raw sugar
½ cup coconut milk
1 tsp salt
4 green onions, thinly sliced

Serves 4

1. Wash the lentils multiple times and then soak them in cold water for about 30 minutes. Strictly speaking, red lentils don't usually need soaking - check your packet for instructions on how to prepare and cook the brand you buy - but I find it reduces foaming.

2. Put the lentils in a large pan with the water. Bring to the boil then reduce the heat and simmer, partially covered, for about 5 minutes, skimming foam off the top as it forms.

3. Stir in the garlic, ginger, onion, green pepper, cayenne, turmeric, garam masala, cardamom and sugar. Bring to the boil then reduce the heat and simmer, partially covered, for about 30 minutes or until the lentils are very tender.

4. Add the coconut milk and salt. Continue to simmer for another 5 minutes then serve topped with green onions.

Red Lentil Chilli

Red lentil chilli is cheap, easy and totally delicious. It is the perfect antidote to a cold, damp day, and you can freeze any leftovers. Serve with rice, hot cornbread muffins or dolloped on top of tortilla chips. It takes a while to cook, but it's totally worth the effort.

2 cups red lentils
3 cups water
2 tsp cumin
1 tsp paprika
½ tsp ground thyme
1 tsp cayenne pepper, or to taste
1 can (28oz) diced tomatoes

1 large onion, finely chopped
6 cloves of garlic, finely chopped
1 tsp salt
1 tsp ground black pepper
4 tbsp tomato paste
1 tbsp balsamic or red wine vinegar

Serves 4

1. Wash the lentils multiple times and then soak them in cold water for 30 minutes.
2. Put the lentils in a large pan with 3 cups of water. Bring to the boil then reduce the heat and simmer, partially covered, for about 30 minutes or until the lentils are tender. If foam forms on top of the soup, carefully skim it off and throw it away.
3. Add the cumin, paprika, thyme, cayenne, tomatoes, onion and garlic and simmer, partially covered, for another 40 minutes. Stir every 15 minutes to make sure it is not sticking to the bottom of the pan. Add more water periodically if needed.
4. Add the salt, black pepper and tomato paste. Simmer for 30 more minutes, stirring occasionally, or until the lentils are very soft. Stir in the vinegar, cook for a final 5 minutes, then serve hot.

Red Lentils with Eggplant

The whole chillies in this curry don't add as much of a kick as you might expect. The lentils tone down the heat considerably.

1 ½ cups red lentils
1 ¼ cups water
1 tsp turmeric
3 jalapeno chillies, halved lengthways
½ large eggplant, cut into thin strips
1 can (28 oz) diced tomatoes
¼ cup water
3 tbsp vegetable oil

1 large onion, thinly sliced
2 garlic cloves, thinly sliced
2 tbsp ginger, finely chopped
1 tsp cumin seeds
1 tsp fennel seeds
1 tsp mustard seeds
1 tsp salt

Serves 4

1. Wash the lentils multiple times and then soak them in cold water for about 30 minutes. Strictly speaking, red lentils don't usually need soaking - check your packet for instructions on how to prepare and cook the brand you buy - but I find it reduces foaming.
2. Put the lentils in a medium pan with 1 ¼ cups of water. Bring to the boil then reduce the heat and simmer, partially covered, for 10 minutes. The lentils will absorb most of the water. If foam forms on top of the lentils, skim it off and throw it away.

3. Stir in the turmeric, chillies, eggplant, tomatoes and ¼ cup of water. Bring to the boil then partially cover and simmer gently for 30 minutes or until the lentils are very soft.
4. Heat the oil in a frying pan and cook the onions, garlic and ginger with the cumin seeds, fennel seeds and mustard seeds over a medium heat for about 10 minutes, or until the onions are golden brown. Stir in the salt and add to the lentils.

Urad Dhal with Rice

If you want, you can cook the rice along with the lentils. Use 2 cups of uncooked rice and 4 ½ cups of water. I prefer to cook my rice separately in my trusty rice cooker so that if my lentils take longer to cook than expected the rice doesn't get soggy.

1 cup white split urad dhal
2 tbsp vegetable oil
1 large onion, finely chopped
2 tbsp grated fresh ginger
1 large carrot, peeled and grated
2 jalapeno chillies, finely chopped
1 tsp cumin
½ tsp ground fenugreek (methi)
2 bay leaves
½ tsp cinnamon

1 tsp turmeric
1 cup green beans, trimmed and chopped
1 tsp salt
3 cups water

3 cups hot basmati rice (cooked with 1 tsp turmeric and 1 tsp cumin)

Serves 4

1. Wash the urad dhal multiple times and then soak them in cold water for 30 minutes - 1 hour. (Check your packet for specific instructions on how to prepare and cook the brand you buy.) Rinse again and drain.
2. Heat the oil in a medium pan and cook the onion, ginger, carrot and chillies over a medium heat for about 10 minutes or until the onion is soft and golden brown.

3. Stir in the lentils, cumin, fenugreek, bay leaves, cinnamon, turmeric, green beans, salt and water. Bring to the boil, reduce the heat, cover and simmer gently for 30 minutes or until the lentils are soft.
4. If there is any excess liquid, drain it off. Mix the lentils with the hot cooked rice and serve.

Yellow Split Peas with Cashews

I usually buy pre-cooked yellow split peas in a can, but occasionally I cook dry ones. They don't need soaking and usually take somewhere between 30 minutes and an hour to cook depending on how old they are. Wash them well before cooking and use a ratio of 1 cup of split peas to 2 cups of water.

2 tbsp olive oil
1 medium onion, finely chopped
2 garlic cloves, finely chopped
1 green chilli, finely chopped
1 leek, finely chopped
2 cups cooked yellow split peas
½ cup water
1 tsp salt
¼ tsp freshly ground black pepper

Final fry:
3 tbsp vegetable oil
1 garlic clove, thinly sliced
½ cup roasted un-salted cashews, chopped
1 tbsp grated fresh ginger
1 jalapeno chilli, thinly sliced
½ cup fresh coriander, finely chopped

Serves 4

1. Heat the olive oil in a large heavy-based pan. Add the onion and cook over a high heat for 2 minutes. Add the garlic and cook for another minute. Stir in the chilli and leek and cook over a medium heat for 5 minutes or until the vegetables have softened.

2. Add the cooked split peas, water, salt and pepper. Bring to the boil (watch out for it spitting out of the pan), reduce the heat to low and simmer very gently for 5 minutes. Add more water if it is too thick.

3. For the final fry, heat the oil in a small frying pan. When hot, add the garlic and cook until golden brown - about 3 minutes. Add the cashews and ginger and cook for another 30 seconds. Pour over the split peas - it should be hot enough to spit - and stir in the coriander.

A Few Words About Seitan, Tempeh and Tofu

Seitan and tempeh are vegan proteins which can be used as "meat substitutes". You can buy tempeh products in some large supermarkets and many natural food stores. Seitan can be a bit harder to find but if you want to try making some at home it's not too difficult. I've not included these proteins in recipes in this book but feel free to use them instead of tofu or faux meats.

Seitan is a meat-like protein made from wheat gluten. It's *not* suitable for people on a gluten-free diet! It originated in Asia where Buddhist monks have been eating it for centuries. Making seitan is a fairly simple but time-consuming process. Whole wheat flour and water are mixed together to form a firm dough, then left soaking in cold water overnight. It's then washed and kneaded until the water runs clear, removing the starch and leaving behind the gluten. This is then squeezed very tightly to remove water and air bubbles before being sliced and dropped into boiling, well-flavoured vegan stock and cooked for about half an hour. The result is a grey-brown product that can be fried, baked or used in soups and stews.

Tempeh is another vegan protein option which is starting to make an appearance in my local stores. It always seems to be in some marinade or other, and is a bit of an acquired taste - kind of nutty with a nougat-like texture. It originated in Asia and is made from slightly fermented soya beans squashed into a firm block. It can be used instead of tofu or faux meats in soups, stews, curries and chillies. By all means buy some and try it in a recipe instead of tofu – it tastes better than it sounds!

Tofu is made from soya beans and a coagulant. It has a very mild taste and absorbs the flavours of sauces and marinades. This can be maximised by wrapping firm tofu in kitchen paper and sitting a heavy plate on top of it to squeeze out excess water before adding it to a recipe. The less water there is in the tofu, the more marinade it can absorb.

Tofu

I've met a number of people who say they've tried tofu and really didn't like it. When asked how they cooked it, the response was invariably "I didn't cook it. I just took it out of the package and ate it." Yuk. No wonder they didn't like it! Much better ideas are to coat extra firm tofu in corn starch and fry until crispy, or marinade firm tofu with ginger, garlic and spices to put in a curry, or put semi-firm tofu in soups and stews, or blend soft tofu with fresh fruit or melted vegan chocolate to make a dessert... but don't just take it out of the box and eat it. Please.

Firm / extra firm tofu - great for frying and soups or stews.

Semi-firm / regular tofu - can be fried if handled carefully. Good in soups.

Soft / silken tofu - great for blending into sauces, dips and desserts.

Black Pepper Tofu

Don't let the boring title of this dish deceive you - it's a feisty little number. Either grind the pepper using your pepper mill or crush the peppercorns using a pestle and mortar or a spice grinder. Don't use the finely-ground black pepper found in shakers.

Tofu:
800g / 1 ¾ lb firm tofu (usually 2 packets)
¼ cup corn starch
6 tbsp vegetable oil

Sauce:
4 tbsp vegetable oil
12 green onions, thinly sliced
12 garlic cloves, finely chopped
3 tbsp finely chopped fresh ginger
2 jalapeno chillies, finely chopped
1 red pepper, cut into bite-size pieces
½ cup soy sauce
2 tbsp raw unrefined sugar
3 - 5 tbsp crushed black peppercorns
6 green onions, cut into chunks

Serves 4

1. Cut the tofu into 1" cubes and pat dry. Coat in corn starch and set aside.
2. Heat 6 tbsp oil in a large frying pan. Add the tofu a few squares at a time and fry all the sides until golden brown - this will take about 5 minutes. Remove from the pan and put on kitchen paper to drain.
3. Clean and dry the pan, add 4 tbsp vegetable oil and fry the chopped green onions, garlic, ginger, chillies and pepper over a low heat for about 5 minutes. Add the soy sauce, sugar and black pepper. Stir well, then add the tofu. Cook for a couple of minutes to reheat the tofu then serve over steamed rice topped with green onion pieces.

Paprika Tofu with Chillies and Lime

This isn't a dish for the faint of heart or tame of stomach. I use more chillies than suggested in the recipe because I like my food HOT. Go ahead and add more chillies according to your personal comfort level. You can serve this dumped onto a mound of salad greens or freshly cooked kale, or simply with a bowl of freshly cooked rice.

Don't forget to add the lime juice. It cuts through the richness of the dish and adds a bit of "zing".

6 tbsp olive oil
6 jalapeno chillies (or more), finely chopped
8 garlic cloves, finely chopped
2 tsp paprika
2 tsp salt
800g / 1 ¾ lb firm or semi-firm tofu, cubed
1 red pepper, coarsely chopped
Juice of 2 limes

Serves 4

1. Heat the oil in a frying pan. Add the chillies and garlic cloves. Cook over a high heat for 1 - 2 minutes or until they brown. Take care not to burn them.
2. Add the paprika and salt. Cook for about 30 seconds then add the tofu and red pepper.
3. Cook over a medium heat until the tofu is golden brown and coated in a dusting of browned chillies, garlic and paprika.
4. Squeeze in the lime juice, add more salt if needed and serve immediately.

Sweet and Sour Tofu

Sweet and sour chicken was a favourite of my dad's when I was growing up, and seems to be a staple of many diners sitting in my favourite Chinese restaurant. I've removed the chicken and added fried tofu instead. Feel free to use faux chicken if you prefer.

800g / 1 ¾ lb firm or semi-firm tofu, cubed and patted dry
4 tbsp corn starch
¼ tsp salt and ¼ tsp ground black pepper
4 tbsp vegetable oil

For the sauce:
2 tbsp vegetable oil
3 tsp fresh ginger, coarsely chopped
2 garlic cloves, coarsely chopped
1 small onion, chopped
1 red or orange pepper, chopped
1 green pepper, chopped
1 cup fresh or canned pineapple chunks, drained with 1/2 cup reserved juice
4 green onions, cut into chunks
3 tbsp raw unrefined sugar
3 tbsp rice wine vinegar
1 tbsp soy sauce
¼ cup vegan "chicken flavour" stock
1 tbsp corn starch mixed with 1 tbsp water

Serves 4
1. **For the tofu**: Toss the tofu with the corn starch, salt and pepper.
2. In a large frying pan, heat the oil and fry the tofu over a medium-high heat for 5 - 10 minutes or until golden brown. Remove the tofu to some kitchen paper and discard the oil.
3. **For the sauce**: Put 2 tbsp oil in the frying pan and stir fry the ginger, garlic, onion and peppers for 5 minutes over a high heat. Add the tofu, pineapple, juice, green onions, sugar, vinegar, soy sauce and stock. Bring to the boil then add the corn starch and water, stirring constantly. Boil for 2 -3 minutes or until thick. Serve immediately with rice.

Tofu with Bok Choy

Shiitake mushrooms are fabulously earthy and chewy. Soak in warm water for 30 minutes before using.

6 dried shiitake mushrooms
4 tbsp sesame oil
800g / 1 ¾ lb firm tofu, cubed
1 large onion, thinly sliced
8 baby bok choy, broken into individual stalks
225g / 8 oz / 1 can sliced water chestnuts, drained
¼ cup soy sauce
2 tsp sugar

Sauce:
1 tbsp sesame oil
2 garlic cloves, crushed
½ tsp crushed dried red chilli flakes
¼ cup crunchy peanut butter
1 cup coconut milk
2 tbsp hoisin sauce
1 tbsp soy sauce
1 tbsp brown sugar

Serves 4

1. **To make the sauce**, heat the oil in a small pan and add the garlic and chillies. Cook over a medium heat for 2 minutes then stir in the peanut butter, coconut milk, hoisin sauce, soy sauce and brown sugar. Cover and leave over a very low heat while you cook the vegetables.

2. **To make the tofu**: Squeeze the water out of the mushrooms, cut into thin slices and pat dry.

3. Heat the oil in a large frying pan and add the tofu. Fry over a high heat for 3 minutes or until light golden brown. Remove the tofu and drain on kitchen paper.

4. Add the onion to the pan and cook over a medium heat for 5 minutes or until golden brown, adding more oil if needed. Stir in the water chestnuts, mushrooms, soy sauce and sugar.

5. Cook over a medium heat for 5 minutes. Add the bok choy to the sauce. Cover and cook over a low heat for 5 minutes or until the bok choy is soft. Serve with rice or noodles.

Tofu in Curry Sauce

This is a mild curry which is not hot or strongly spiced. Personally, I like mine HOT so I throw in a couple of **chopped jalapeno chillies** along with the tofu.

800g / 1 ¾ lb firm tofu, cubed

Marinade:
6 garlic cloves, crushed
1 tsp grated fresh ginger
3 tsp paprika
1 tbsp dried coriander
1 tbsp cumin
1 tbsp garam masala
½ tsp crushed dried red chilli
1 tsp salt
2 tsp lime juice

Sauce:
5 tbsp vegetable oil
1 cup coconut milk
4 large tomatoes, coarsely chopped
2 tbsp tomato paste
10 curry (methi) leaves
½ tsp paprika
¼ tsp white wine vinegar
½ tsp garam masala
1 tsp salt or to taste
Handful fresh coriander (optional)

Serves 4

1. In a resealable plastic bag, mix together the tofu, garlic, ginger, paprika, coriander, cumin, garam masala, chilli, salt and lime juice. Leave in the fridge for at least an hour or, if possible, overnight.
2. Heat the oil in a large frying pan. Add the tofu and marinade and cook over a medium-high heat for 5 minutes.
3. Add the coconut milk, tomatoes, tomato paste and curry leaves. Bring to the boil, reduce the heat, cover and simmer gently for 30 minutes, removing the lid for the final 10 minutes to allow the sauce to thicken slightly.
4. Stir in the paprika, vinegar, garam masala and salt. Serve sprinkled with fresh coriander.

Tofu in Simplified Mole Poblano

Variations: Use a combination of white, portabella and shiitake mushrooms instead of the tofu. Fry in a little olive oil and drain off the liquid before adding to the sauce. Or use sliced, cooked "faux chicken breasts". They both work well instead of tofu.

2 tbsp olive oil
1 medium onion, chopped
3 garlic cloves, chopped
1 canned chipotle pepper
2 tsp adobo sauce from can
1 cup raisins
1 cup canned diced tomatoes
2 tsp cayenne powder
½ tsp ground cinnamon
6 cloves, ground
½ tsp fennel seeds, ground

½ tsp ground allspice
½ tsp cumin
1 tsp freshly ground black pepper
½ ripe banana, mashed
2 cups vegan "chicken flavour" stock
2 tsp salt
2 tbsp cocoa powder
800g / 1 ¾ lb thinly sliced firm tofu
Soft tortillas for serving

Serves 4

1. Heat the oil in a large pan and add the onion and garlic. Cook over a medium heat for 10 minutes or until soft and slightly golden.
2. Add the chipotle, adobo, raisins, tomatoes, cayenne, cinnamon, cloves, fennel, allspice, cumin, black pepper and mashed banana. Bring to a boil, reduce the heat and simmer, uncovered, for 10 minutes.
3. Carefully pour the mixture into a blender and blend until smooth. Add the stock and salt.
4. Return the mixture to the pan and simmer for 15 minutes, stirring occasionally. Add the cocoa and cook for another 5 minutes. Stir in the sliced tofu and heat through.
5. Wrap the tofu and some sauce in soft tortillas and drizzle a put extra sauce over the top.

Tofu with Satay Sauce

The sauce is very easy to make in the blender, or you can just mix it together in a bowl.

2 packs firm tofu, cubed
¼ cup soy sauce
1 tsp grated lemon rind
4 garlic cloves, crushed
230g / 8oz rice noodles
Large pot of boiling water
2 tbsp vegetable oil
2 cups grated carrots
2 cups beansprouts
1 cup thinly sliced snow peas

Sauce: Mix together:
1 ¼ cups coconut milk
¾ cup crunchy peanut butter
4 tbsp soy sauce
3 tbsp fresh ginger, finely chopped
3 tbsp unrefined raw sugar
1 tsp crushed dried red chillies
¼ cup fresh basil or mint

Garnish:
Baby greens (optional)

Serves 4

1. Put the cubed tofu in a re-sealable plastic bag. Add the soy sauce, lemon rind and crushed garlic and set aside. This can be left in the fridge overnight if you like.
2. Soak the rice noodles in hot water for 5 minutes, or as per instructions on the packet. Drain.
3. Heat the oil in a large frying pan. Pat the tofu dry and place it in the pan. Cook over a medium-high heat for 5 minutes or until it starts to turn golden brown. Reduce the heat to low and cook gently for 15 minutes.
4. Add the carrots, beansprouts and snow peas. Cook for 1 minute or until hot.
5. Stir in the sauce and, stirring constantly, heat without boiling. Serve on top of the noodles sprinkled and garnished with baby salad greens.

A Few Words About Gluten-Free Cooking

Eating a gluten-free diet has nothing to do with being vegan, but I thought it was worth putting a little note about it because so many people have an intolerance to gluten. Celiac disease is not the same as gluten intolerance, but both require a gluten-free diet. There are some useful websites including **www.celiac.ca** and **http://glutenfreenetwork.com**

Some commonly used products to avoid (not a complete list) are:

- Anything that has wheat in the name. This includes cracked wheat, whole wheat, wheat starch, wheat germ, wheat bran, bulgur wheat and durum wheat (semolina).
- Cooked or dried cereals made from or containing wheat. Read the ingredients - even some cornflakes contain wheat or maltodextrin, which *may* be made from wheat.
- Wheat bread or bread products. I buy gluten-free bread from the health food section of my local grocery store - it's usually in the freezer. I find quinoa bread is good for making breadcrumbs.
- Cooked or dry pasta or couscous made with wheat. There are now many gluten free varieties available, including corn couscous, and they're actually rather nice.
- Any matzo product. I've never bought matzo, so I can't suggest a substitute.
- Cookies and cakes made with wheat. I use Pamela's or Red Mills gluten-free all purpose flour to make gluten-free cakes and cookies. They taste more "wholesome" than standard all purpose flour and have a bit of a chalky texture, but they're not bad.
- Tempeh, which isn't included in any of my recipes, may contain wheat.
- Some vegan faux meats may have wheat as one of the ingredients.
- Stock cubes, commercial vinegars, salad dressings, some soy sauces, some ketchups and vegan mayonnaise may contain wheat. I use McCormick's all vegetable stock cubes and Kikkoman brand soy sauce, but *always* check the label and research products before using them.
- Some beers and ale contain wheat.

Some brands of faux meat contain wheat or other forms of gluten. Read the ingredients on the package carefully if you or someone you are cooking for has an allergy or an intolerance.

Faux Meat

I don't often use meat or chicken look-alikes, but I thought I'd include a few recipes in case you want to try them. Do note that **some vegans won't eat faux meat because it looks too much like the real thing**. My local grocery store carries frozen **vegan "chicken breasts"** and **vegan "cubed beef"** as well as a variety of fresh and frozen **ground meat substitutes**. Chinese supermarkets can be a good source of faux meat products, as can some natural / health food stores. Wherever you get faux meat from, always read the ingredients carefully to check for **egg** or **dairy products**.

If you want to make traditional ground meat dishes into vegan-friendly versions, simply use veggie grounds instead of ground meat. For example, if you want to make a spaghetti bolognaise simply fry up some veggie grounds with the onions and garlic, along with any other vegetables you fancy such as thinly sliced celery or carrots. Add a vegan stock cube, the pasta sauce and herbs, bring to the boil, cover and simmer gently for 40 minutes or until the vegetables are cooked.

It's very simple to replace the ground meat or chicken in your favourite recipes with the vegan alternatives, but remember to check that all the other ingredients in your recipe are also vegan. Don't go adding a dash of Worcestershire sauce or a teaspoon of honey! And remember, you wouldn't expect an artificial "crab stick" to have the same taste and texture as real crab, so don't expect vegan "chicken" to taste and feel like the feathered variety. Enjoy it for what it is - a healthy, vegan-friendly, cruelty-free addition to the dinner table.

A note to cooks in the UK and the USA - the vegetarian meat replacement "Quorn" (at the time of writing this) is not suitable for vegans as it contains egg. However, the manufacturers of Quorn have produced a vegan-friendly burger and more egg-free products are expected to follow. I suggest you read the ingredients list on the box.

"Chicken Breasts" in Chipotle Sauce

If you can't find vegetarian "chicken" in your local grocery or natural food stores, use slices of firm tofu instead.

Four chipotle and two tablespoons of sauce are all you need to make this dish, unless you like things *really* hot. Pop the remains of the can in a small plastic box and freeze for another day.

4 tbsp olive oil
1 large onion, finely chopped
6 garlic cloves, crushed
2 tsp cumin
4 chipotle chillies, finely chopped
2 tbsp adobe sauce from the chipotle can

¼ tsp ground black pepper
1 tsp salt
1 can (28 oz) diced tomatoes
1 bay leaf
½ cup fresh coriander, chopped
4 vegan "chicken" breasts

Serves 4

1. Heat the olive oil in a large pan and fry the onion and garlic over a medium heat for 10 minutes or until softened but not browned. Add the cumin, chipotles and adobe sauce and continue to cook for a couple of minutes.
2. Add the pepper, salt, tomatoes, bay leaf and coriander. Mix well.
3. Put the "chicken" in the pan and stir to coat with sauce. Cook according to the packet instructions - mine cook from frozen for 15 - 20 minutes.
4. Serve with rice and a fresh salad.

"Chicken" Vindaloo

This is based on a vindaloo curry, but I have greatly reduced the amount of chillies in it. If you want to burn your taste buds off, go ahead and add 15 - 20 whole red chillies.

Marinade:
5 dried red chillies, finely chopped
1 tsp cumin
½ tsp ground cloves
½ tsp cinnamon
1 tsp ground black pepper
1 star anise, crushed
2 tbsp grated fresh ginger
6 garlic cloves, crushed
1 tbsp tamarind pulp
4 tsp cider vinegar

1/3 cup vegetable oil
1 large onion, thinly sliced
4 vegan "chicken breasts"
4 medium potatoes, cut into 8
3 cups water
4 tbsp tomato paste
½ tsp unrefined raw sugar
15 dried curry (methi) leaves
1 tsp salt
2 cups okra (optional), trimmed slightly
¼ cup fresh coriander, chopped

Serves 4

1. Mix together the chillies, cumin, cloves, cinnamon, pepper, star anise, ginger, garlic, tamarind and vinegar. Rub onto the "chicken" and leave for 20 minutes.
2. In a large saucepan, heat the oil and fry the onion over a high heat for 15 minutes or until very browned. Add the "chicken" and marinade along with the potatoes and cook over a medium heat for 5 minutes, turning occasionally.
3. Add the water, tomato paste, sugar, curry leaves and salt. Mix well, bring to the boil, cover, reduce the heat and simmer for 30 minutes or until the potatoes are cooked and tender.
4. If using okra, add to the curry 10 minutes before the end of the cooking time. Serve topped with coriander.

"Chicken" Pot Pie

When I did a quick survey of what friends would serve if they had someone for dinner, Sue (a Canadian who emigrated from England) said "chicken pot pie". I would never have thought of serving a pie, but thanks to Sue, here is a not-chicken pot pie. When I served it for supper we were suspicious at first (we eat a lot of curries, chillies and Asian food) but it was so fabulous that we all went back for more.

Adjust the seasoning according to how well flavoured your vegan stock is. Some brands are fine while others are quite pathetic.

2 tbsp olive oil
1 medium onion, finely chopped
2 leeks, cleaned and chopped
2 medium carrots, scrubbed and thinly sliced
2 cloves garlic, crushed
4 vegan "chicken" breasts
2 medium potatoes, peeled if you want, cut into ¼-inch chunks
2 tbsp dried parsley
1 tbsp dried oregano
1 tbsp dried basil
1 ½ tsp salt
¼ tsp ground black pepper
1 tbsp vegan margarine
4 cups vegan "chicken" stock
2 tbsp corn starch mixed with 2 tbsp water
200g frozen puff pastry, thawed at room temperature for 2 hours (check the ingredients)

Serves 4

1. Heat the oven to 375'F /190'C / Gas Mark 5 - you will need it to be ready 45 minutes after you start cooking the filling.
2. Heat the oil in a medium sized pan and fry the onion, leeks, carrots and garlic for about 5 minutes or until slightly softened.

3. Add the chicken, potatoes, parsley, oregano, basil, salt, pepper and stock. Bring to a boil then reduce to a low simmer, cover and cook for 40 - 45 minutes.

4. Remove the "chicken" and shred into pieces. Using a spoon with holes in it, transfer the potatoes and vegetables to an oven-proof dish. Add the chicken.

5. Transfer 2 cups of the cooking liquid into a small pan along with 1 tbsp vegan margarine. Add the corn starch and water and, stirring constantly, bring to the boil. Continue to stir until it thickens, about 1 - 2 minutes, then pour over the chicken and potatoes.

6. Roll out the pastry to just larger than the dish and place on top of the stew. Trim the edges and cut 3 small slits in the top for venting. Place the dish on a tray to catch drips and bake for 40 - 50 minutes or until the pasty is golden brown and you can see gravy bubbling through the vent slits.

7. Allow to sit for 10 minutes before serving with vegetables of your choice.

Chinese Veggie Grounds with Lettuce

Soya grounds are great cooked with chillies and garlic then wrapped in lettuce leaves. You can also serve it mixed into freshly cooked rice. Hoisin sauce is available in most grocery stores or Asian supermarkets. It's usually vegan but always read the ingredients before you buy it. If you want to make this dish more substantial, soak some rice noodles in hot water for 5 minutes (or according to the directions on the packet), drain and wrap in the lettuce with the spiced "meat".

2 tbsp vegetable oil
6 garlic cloves, coarsely chopped
3 tbsp fresh ginger, coarsely chopped
6 green onions, thinly sliced
2 tsp crushed dried red chillies
450g / 1 lb veggie grounds
3 tbsp soy sauce
4 tbsp sake or sherry

4 tbsp hoisin sauce
2 tsp salt
3 tsp unrefined raw sugar
4 tbsp water
2 tbsp lime juice
½ cup chopped fresh mint, basil or coriander
Fresh lettuce leaves to serve

Serves 4

1. In a large frying pan, heat the oil then stir fry the garlic, ginger and onions for 1 minute. Add the red chillies and veggie grounds and cook for another minute.
2. Add the soy sauce, sake, hoisin sauce, salt, sugar and water. Stir fry for 5 minutes over a medium heat.
3. Stir in the lime juice and mint. Either serve hot or allow to cool to room temperature, wrapped in lettuce leaves.

Shepherdless Pie with Baked Beans

This is a vegan remake of the old classic British dish of ground lamb topped with buttered potatoes. I love **Original Heinz Baked Beans**, which are usually vegan - as long as they aren't the varieties containing **pork** or **lard**, of course! Make sure you buy the right one!

3 tbsp olive oil
1 large onion, finely chopped
2 garlic cloves, finely chopped
450g / 1 lb veggie grounds
1 can Heinz Baked Beans in tomato sauce
2 tbsp tomato paste
½ can (28oz) diced tomatoes
1 tsp dried oregano
1 tsp dried basil
2 tsp dried parsley
1 tsp salt
½ tsp ground black pepper

Topping:
4 medium potatoes, peeled and quartered
Large pan boiling water
2 tbsp vegan margarine

Serves 4

1. Heat the oven to 400'F / 200'C / Gas Mark 6.
2. Heat the oil in a frying pan and cook the onion and garlic over a medium heat for 5 minutes or until soft. Stir in the veggie grounds, baked beans, tomato paste, diced tomatoes, oregano, basil, parsley, salt and pepper. Bring to a boil then reduce the heat, cover and simmer gently for 30 minutes.
3. Put the potatoes in a large pan of boiling water and simmer for 20 minutes or until soft. Drain and mash with the margarine.
4. Transfer the sauce to a large oven-proof dish (about 9" x 13") and top with the mashed potatoes. Bake for 30 minutes.

Simple Veggie Grounds Chilli with Cornbread Muffins

In order for this dish to taste fabulous you need to have a good pre-mixed chilli powder. Don't buy generic or no-name brands - they really aren't worth the money. Adjust the quantity according to how hot your mix is.

Chilli:
3 tbsp olive oil
1 medium onion, finely chopped
4 garlic cloves, finely chopped
4 tbsp good quality chili powder
2 tsp cumin
225g / 8 oz veggie grounds
1 (28 oz) can diced tomatoes
1 tbsp dried oregano
1 tsp salt
½ tsp ground black pepper
2 tbsp tomato paste
1 can / 2 cups cooked black beans

Serves 4

Muffins:
2 tbsp olive oil
1 cup finely chopped red pepper
1 cup organic flour
1 cup corn meal
2 tbsp raw unrefined sugar
2 ½ tsp baking powder
¼ tsp baking soda
¼ tsp salt
4 tbsp unsweetened applesauce
1 cup soy milk

Makes 12 standard or 6 jumbo muffins

1. Heat the oil in a large frying pan and cook the onions and garlic over a medium heat for 5 minutes, then add the chilli powder and cumin. Stir for 1 minute then add the veggie grounds and mix well.
2. Add the tomatoes, oregano, salt, black pepper and tomato paste. Mix well, bring to the boil, reduce the heat, cover and simmer gently for 40 minutes. Check the seasoning half way through and add more chilli powder if needed. Too hot? Add 1 tsp sugar.
3. Stir in the beans and continue to cook for another 10 minutes and serve with tortilla chips, rice or vegan cornbread muffins.
4. To make the muffins, heat the oven to 400'F / 200'C / Gas Mark 6.
5. In a small frying pan, heat the oil and fry the peppers over a medium heat for about 10 minutes, or until soft. Alternatively, put in the microwave for 3 minutes. Allow to cool.
6. Lightly grease a muffin tray or line with paper cases.
7. In a large bowl, mix together the flour, corn meal, sugar, baking powder, baking soda and salt.

8. Stir in the applesauce and soy milk, then stir in the red pepper with its juices and remaining oil. Mix until just blended. Put into the muffin tray and bake for 20 - 25 minutes or until a toothpick inserted in the center comes out clean.

9. Allow to cool in the pan for 10 minutes before serving.

A Word About Vegan Dairy Substitutes

You may have noticed a lack of cheesy dishes in this book, which is partly due to the fact that many vegetarian cheeses still contain **casein**. I can't understand why someone would eat something that tastes like a cardboard box but still contains animal products. I personally don't cook with cheese, regardless of whether it's the real deal or something vegan which even a very hungry mouse wouldn't touch. However, if you want to add some cheesiness to vegan dishes, there are now some brands appearing on the market which don't contain casein and are nut based rather than soy based. I've not tried them and can only tell you that other people have said they're good. Sprinkling food with nutritional yeast also gives it a cheesy flavour.

As far as **vegan yoghurts, cream cheeses and sour creams** go, I've had various levels of success with them. Soy yoghurt mixed with a pinch of cumin, paprika, salt, chillies and dried mint went down well as a side dish with a curry, but guests didn't like the same dish made using coconut yoghurt. A pleasant herby not-cream-cheese dip can be made using soy based "cream cheese" instead ones made using dairy products.

There are many non-dairy **milk substitutes** on the market, and finding one you like is a matter of trial and error. Some people like a particular brand of **soy** milk but don't like other brands, while some people only like **almond** or **cashew** milk. Me, I'm a **hemp** girl. There are various brands of non-dairy creamers available for putting in coffee. Note that the **coconut milk** for drinking is not the same as the cans of coconut milk used for cooking.

I use **Earth Balance** brand margarine for cooking and baking.

If you use mayonnaise, have a look for vegan varieties such as **Veganaise**.

Nuts

I don't use a lot of nuts in my cooking despite the health benefits associated with them. This is mainly because there is a tree-nut allergy in the family. Having said that, when they do make an appearance I really enjoy them. The nut roast is well worth the time and effort to make. I usually use inexpensive peanuts but you can use any combination of chopped nuts that takes your fancy.

Various types of **nut butters** (cashew, almond, hazelnut, for example) are available in grocery and health food stores. They can be quite expensive but make a nice treat every now and again. They can be used in recipes as a replacement for peanut butter, which is useful if you have a peanut allergy in the house, or spread on apples as a healthy snack.

Natural, unsalted, sugar-free peanut butter, which needs to be refrigerated after opening, is becoming widely available. I know it's the healthier option but I actually prefer regular chunky peanut butter which has added salt and sugar. I like the taste more and the oils don't separate out. I'm told that if you store natural peanut butter upside down you don't have to vigorously stir it every time you want to use it, but I can't be bothered with all that. If a recipe calls for peanut butter, feel free to use whatever type you prefer and add more salt if needed.

I frequently get mocked by my Canadian friends for my pronunciation of CaSHEW nuts. They say it sounds like I'm sneezing. Personally I don't think their version, CAshew nuts, is much of an improvement!

Cabbage and Cashew Nuts

This is a quick and easy vegetarian main dish or a side dish as part of a multi-dish Chinese meal. I buy pre-chopped coleslaw because I'm sometimes quite lazy!

1 tbsp vegetable oil
1 onion, thinly sliced
4 garlic cloves, thinly sliced
2 jalapeno chillies, thinly sliced
6 cups sliced white cabbage
4 dried shiitake mushrooms (soaked in warm water for 30 minutes, squeezed and thinly sliced)
1 tsp sesame oil
1 tsp soy sauce
1 tbsp sake
¼ tsp ground black pepper
1 cup cashew nuts

Serves 4

1. Heat the oil in a large frying pan and cook the onion, garlic and chillies over a high heat for 5 minutes. Add the cabbage and shiitake and continue to fry for another 5 minutes.
2. Stir in the sesame oil, soy sauce, sake and pepper. Reduce the heat and cook gently for 5 minutes.
3. Stir in the cashew nuts and serve immediately.

Cauliflower, Cashew Nut and Green Bean Curry

This curry is so tasty and easy to make that even a dedicated meat eater has asked for the recipe.

2 tbsp vegetable oil
1 onion, finely sliced
4 garlic cloves, finely chopped
1 tbsp fresh ginger, finely chopped
1 or 2 jalapeno chillies, finely chopped
4 - 6 tbsp curry powder
1 tsp salt
1 can of coconut milk
½ cup vegan "chicken flavour" stock
½ cup peanut butter
1 large cauliflower, broken into florets (4 to 6 cups)
2 cups green beans, trimmed and cut into bite size lengths
1 cup roasted unsalted cashew halves or pieces

Serves 4

1. Heat the oil in a large pan and fry the onion, garlic, ginger and chillies over a high heat for 5 minutes. Stir in the curry powder and salt and cook for 30 seconds or until fragrant.
2. Mix in the coconut milk, stock and peanut butter, then add the cauliflower and green beans.
3. Bring to the boil, reduce the heat, cover and simmer gently for 10 - 15 minutes or until the cauliflower is cooked. Don't overcook the cauliflower. You need it to be tender-crisp, not soggy and limp.
4. Stir in the cashew nuts and cook for another minute. Serve with rice.

Peanuts with Enoki Mushrooms

I like to use enoki mushrooms in this tasty dish, but feel free to substitute thinly sliced fresh shiitake, oyster or regular mushrooms, or a combination of them. You can also swap the snow peas and red pepper for other thinly sliced, quick-cooking vegetables such as carrots or asparagus. Don't leave out the chillies though - they're what make the dish exciting.

2 tbsp sesame oil
1 red pepper, thinly sliced
2 cups snow peas, thinly sliced
1 tbsp freshly grated ginger
2 garlic cloves, crushed
3 dried red chillies, thinly sliced
2 cups enoki mushrooms (or other mushrooms, thinly sliced)
2 tbsp hoisin sauce
1 tsp sugar
1 cup unsalted roasted peanuts
1 bunch fresh basil, chopped
5 green onions, thinly sliced

Serves 4

1. Heat the oil in a large frying pan. Add the red pepper, snow peas, ginger, garlic and chillies. Fry for 2 minutes over a high heat.
2. Add the enoki mushrooms and continue to fry for another minute.
3. Stir in the hoisin sauce, sugar and peanuts. Cook for 1 minute.
4. Add the fresh basil and serve immediately, topped with thinly sliced green onions.

Pine Nuts with Mushrooms

This dish can be made with regular white mushrooms, but it's so much better if you use a combination of more exotic mushrooms such as king oyster, cremeni and fresh shiitake. Don't use portabella mushrooms - the flavour is much too strong.

450g / 1 lb pasta
Large pan of boiling water
4 tbsp olive oil
400g / 14 oz mixed mushrooms, thinly sliced
3 garlic cloves, finely chopped
1 red pepper, finely chopped
8 green onions, finely chopped
1 tsp ground ginger
1 tsp paprika

1 tsp ground coriander
1 tsp cinnamon
1 tsp dried crushed red chili
½ tsp turmeric
1 tsp salt
½ cup chopped fresh mint
½ cup chopped fresh parsley
2 tbsp vegan margarine (optional)
½ cup toasted pine nuts

Serves 4

1. Bring a large pan of water to the boil. Add the pasta and boil uncovered for 10 - 12 minutes.
2. As soon as you put the pasta in the boiling water, put the oil in a large frying pan and add the mushrooms, garlic, red pepper and green onions. Fry for 8 minutes over a medium high heat or until soft. Stir in the ginger, paprika, coriander, cinnamon, chili, turmeric and salt. Stir in the mint, parsley and margarine. Allow the margarine to melt over a low heat.
3. Mix together the cooked, drained pasta and the spiced mushrooms. Top with toasted pine nuts and serve immediately.

Vegan Nut Roast with Herb Stuffing and Onion Gravy

Back in England in the 80's nut roasts were all the rage in vegetarian circles. I even had my wedding reception at a carvery that offered beef, turkey, salmon, and... nut roast. Packets of dried nut roast mix were available everywhere and all I had to do was mix them with water and pop them in the oven. I also made my own from scratch, but the trick to vegan cooking is finding ways to stick it all together without using eggs or cheese, or strange sludgy things like soaked chia seeds. I eventually resorted to good old corn starch, which seems to do the trick without any drama.

Nut Roast:
4 tbsp olive oil
2 onions, finely chopped
3 garlic cloves, crushed
2 celery sticks, finely chopped
1 large carrot, grated
1 cup finely chopped roasted unsalted cashews, walnuts, pecans, peanuts, or a mixture
1 cup / ½ can cooked green or brown lentils, rinsed
1 ½ cups stale whole wheat breadcrumbs (you can also use gluten-free breadcrumbs)
1 tsp salt
2 tbsp vegan margarine
2 tbsp fresh parsley, finely chopped, or 1 tsp dried parsley
1 tsp dried crushed red chillies (optional)
2 tbsp corn starch mixed with 2 tbsp of water

Herb Stuffing (optional):
2 cups stale breadcrumbs (you can also use gluten-free breadcrumbs)
4 green onions, finely chopped
1 tsp fresh thyme leaves, finely chopped
1 tsp fresh oregano, finely chopped
2 tbsp fresh parsley, finely chopped
½ cup vegan margarine, melted
1 tbsp corn starch mixed with 2 tbsp water

Onion Gravy:
1 tbsp olive oil
2 large onions, thinly sliced
1 tsp sugar
2 tbsp plain flour (or 1 tbsp corn starch mixed with 2 tbsp water if you're gluten-free)
1 vegan "chicken flavour" stock cube dissolved in 1 ½ cups hot water
½ cup white or red wine (optional)

1. Heat the oven to 375'F / 190'C / Gas Mark 5
2. **To make the nut roast**: Heat the oil in a frying pan and fry the onions, garlic, celery and carrot over a high heat for 10 minutes or until the onions are soft and slightly browned.
3. Add the nuts, lentils, breadcrumbs, salt, margarine, parsley and chillies. Stir until the margarine melts and everything is mixed together. Add the corn starch in water and mix well.
4. **To make the herb stuffing**: Mix together the breadcrumbs, green onions, herbs, margarine and corn starch.
5. Press **half** of the nut roast into an oiled loaf tin. Top with the herb stuffing then cover with the remaining nut roast. Bake for around 45 minutes and until browned on top. Allow to cool for 10 minutes before tipping out onto a plate and serving.
6. **To make the gravy**: Heat the oil in a large frying pan. Add the onions and sprinkle with the sugar. Cook over medium heat, stirring occasionally, for about 15 minutes or until the onion is soft and lightly caramelised.
7. Sprinkle the flour over the onion and stir-fry for 1 minute. Gradually add the stock and wine, stirring constantly. Bring to the boil, then reduce the heat stir until thickened.

If you're willing to give vegan cheese a try, throw in 1 cup of grated cheddar flavour into the nut roast along with everything else.

Want to cheat with the gravy? I have a box of beef flavoured instant Bisto granules in my pantry which is free of animal products. It's really easy to make and tastes great. However, it does contain MSG and wheat so may not be suitable for people sensitive to these items. Check your local store to see what is available.

Vegetable Main Dishes

Sometimes it's nice to let vegetables play the starring role in a meal rather than always being overshadowed by a protein dish. I've stuck to readily available veggies in these recipes but there are a couple of items you may not be familiar with:

Marinated Artichoke Hearts:

I buy artichoke hearts from my local grocery store, but they can also be picked up at Italian or Mediterranean specialty stores. They are usually in cans or glass jars.

Sundried Tomatoes in Oil:

Sundried tomatoes can be found at many supermarkets or Italian grocery stores. They are available simply dried in packets for you to rehydrate or preserved in oil in a jar, which is my preference. They have a rich, almost candied taste to them and are fabulous in pasta sauces, on pizza or in salads.

Apricot and Vegetable Tagine with Harissa

The artichoke hearts and olives are essential to the exotic flavour of this dish, so don't leave them out if you can avoid it.

6 tbsp olive oil
1 large onion, thinly sliced
1 tbsp freshly ground black pepper
2 tsp cumin
1 tsp turmeric
1 tsp cinnamon
1 tsp paprika
3 tbsp water
1 medium eggplant, cubed
2 medium potatoes, peeled and cut into bite-size pieces
1 large carrot, peeled and thinly sliced
1 red pepper, cut into large pieces
1 green pepper, cut into large pieces
1 tsp salt
2 jars (170ml each) artichoke hearts, rinsed and drained

1 can (28 oz) diced tomatoes
1 tbsp tomato paste
1 cup freshly chopped parsley
½ cup dried apricots, left whole or diced
½ cup pitted olives

Harissa:
Mix together the following:
¼ cup olive oil
4 garlic cloves, crushed
1 tsp salt
1 tbsp cumin
2 tsp caraway seeds
¼ cup dried red chillies, crushed

Serves 4

1. Heat the oil in a large saucepan. Fry the onion over a medium heat until soft, about 5 minutes.
2. Mix the freshly ground black pepper, cumin, turmeric, cinnamon and paprika together with enough water to make a paste. Add to the pan and fry for about 2 minutes or until fragrant.
3. Add the eggplant, potatoes, carrot, red pepper, green pepper and salt. Cook until the eggplant starts to soften, about 5 minutes.
4. Add the artichoke hearts, tomatoes and tomato paste along with enough water to just cover the vegetables if needed. Cover and simmer for 50 min - 1 hour or until the potatoes and carrots are tender.
5. Stir in the parsley, apricots and olives. Cook for 5 minutes then serve with couscous, quinoa, rice or bread. Add harissa to taste.

Cauliflower Curry

Overcooked cauliflower is truly awful, so make sure you cook this curry until it's tender but still has a bit of a bite to it. Don't forget to add the lemon juice at the end - it really adds to the taste.

4 tbsp vegetable oil
6 cloves garlic, crushed
2 tbsp grated fresh ginger
1 jalapeno chilli, finely chopped
1 finely chopped onion
1 tbsp ground coriander
1 tsp cumin
½ tsp turmeric
2 tsp salt
3 tbsp water
1 large cauliflower, broken into florets
1 cup coconut milk
½ cup fresh coriander
½ cup fresh mint
2 tbsp lemon juice

Serves 4

1. In a large frying pan, heat the oil and fry the garlic, ginger, chilli and onion over a medium-high heat until lightly browned, about 10 minutes.
2. Add the coriander, cumin, turmeric and salt along with the water. Fry for 2 minutes.
3. Add the cauliflower and coconut milk, cover and simmer on low heat for 20 minutes.
4. Stir in the fresh coriander, mint and lemon juice. Serve immediately.

Eggplant with Black Bean Sauce

You can use thin Chinese eggplants for this dish or the regular large purple ones. If you want to add a bit of texture or taste variation, throw in some roasted unsalted peanuts or cashew nuts. **Black bean sauce** is available in most grocery stores or Asian supermarkets. Check the ingredients, but they're usually vegan.

2 tbsp vegetable oil
1 medium onion, thinly sliced
4 garlic cloves, finely chopped
3 jalapeno chillies, deseeded and finely chopped
2 large eggplants, thinly sliced
1 red pepper, coarsely chopped
½ tsp salt
3 tbsp mirin or sweet wine

2 tbsp unrefined raw sugar
2 tbsp soy sauce
1 tbsp lime juice
2 tbsp water
3 tbsp black bean sauce
8 green onions, finely chopped
¼ cup fresh mint leaves, chopped
1 cup roasted unsalted cashew nuts (optional)

Serves 4

1. Heat the oil in a large frying pan and cook the onion over a medium heat for 10 minutes or until soft. Add the garlic, chillies, eggplants and pepper and cook for another 5 minutes.
2. Stir in the salt, mirin, sugar, soy sauce, lime juice, water, black bean sauce and green onions. Bring to the boil then reduce the heat, cover and simmer very gently for 15 - 20 minutes or until the eggplant is very soft.
3. Stir in the cashew nuts (if using) and mint, cook for 2 minutes then serve hot.

Marinated Vegetables with Pasta

This dish requires planning ahead to give the vegetables plenty of time to marinate.

2 red peppers (or yellow or orange)
1 small eggplant
1 large zucchini
20 baby mushrooms or 10 large mushrooms, sliced
20 cherry tomatoes, halved
1 jar (170ml) artichoke hearts in marinade
¼ red onion, finely chopped

½ cup fresh parsley, chopped
¼ cup fresh basil, chopped
4 garlic cloves, finely chopped
½ tsp salt
6 tbsp olive oil
2 tbsp red wine or balsamic vinegar
20 small olives, or 10 sliced large olives
450g / 1 lb pasta
Large pan of boiling water

Serves 4

1. **The day before dinner**, heat the oven to 450'F / 230'C / Gas Mark 8, put the peppers, eggplant and zucchini on a baking sheet covered in foil and bake for 45 minutes or until the peppers are charred and the eggplant is soft and shriveled. When cool, remove the skins and seeds from the peppers.

2. Slice the eggplant, zucchini and peppers. Put into a large re-sealable plastic bag with the mushrooms, tomatoes, artichoke hearts (along with the marinade from the jar), onion, parsley, basil, garlic, salt, olive oil, vinegar and olives. Put in the fridge and leave until the next day.

3. **When you are ready for dinner**, bring a large pot of water to the boil and cook the pasta for 10 -12 minutes.

4. Just before the pasta has finished cooking, put the marinade and vegetables in a pan or in the microwave and warm gently.

5. Drain the pasta and toss with the warm vegetables. Serve immediately.

Potato Curry with Spinach

I have to admit that I don't like potatoes. It doesn't matter if they're boiled, deep fried, baked, spiced, curried or mashed - I simply don't like them. If you're waiting for me to say "but I love them in this dish" I'm afraid you're going to be disappointed, but everyone else seems to enjoy a portion of lightly spiced potatoes next to a lentil or tofu curry.

4 - 6 medium potatoes, quartered
½ tsp turmeric
Water
2 tbsp vegetable oil
1 tsp yellow mustard seeds
2 large tomatoes, chopped
1 large onion, finely chopped
8 curry leaves

1 tsp salt
1 tsp fennel seeds
2 tsp cumin seeds
1 tsp dried crushed red chillies
3 garlic cloves, crushed
1 large bunch of spinach, washed
Juice of 1 lemon

Serves 4

1. Put the potatoes and turmeric in a large pan with enough water to cover. Bring to the boil and simmer, covered, for 20 minutes or until the potatoes are tender. Drain and coarsely chop.

2. Heat the oil in a large frying pan. Add the mustard seeds and fry until they crackle. Watch out - they can pop and jump out of the pan. Reduce the heat and add the tomatoes, onion and curry leaves. Fry until the onion is soft, about 10 minutes on a medium heat.

3. Add the salt, fennel seeds, cumin seeds, chillies and garlic. Mix in the potatoes and a small amount of water. Cover and allow the potatoes to heat though for 5 minutes.

4. Add the spinach, in batches if necessary, and allow it to wilt. Squeeze in the lemon juice and serve hot.

Roasted Pepper and Sundried Tomato Salad or Pasta

This dish can be used two ways - make a salad or a pasta dish, depending on your mood.

4 large red or yellow peppers
2 tbsp capers
½ cup sliced green and/or black olives

Dressing:
½ cup sun-dried tomatoes, (rehydrated if dry,) finely chopped
2 tbsp fresh basil
2 garlic cloves, crushed
2 tbsp balsamic vinegar
½ cup olive oil

Option 1: Salad
4 cups mixed salad greens
¼ cup toasted pine nuts

Option 2: Pasta
4 cups freshly cooked pasta
1 tsp crushed chili flakes
1 tsp salt

Serves 4

1. Put the peppers on a baking tray and put them in a hot (450'F / 230'C / Gas Mark 8) oven for 45 minutes. Allow to cool very briefly and then put in a plastic bag to cool completely. The charred skins should then just slide off.
2. Remove the stems and seeds then slice the peppers into thick strips.
3. Toss the peppers with the capers and olives.
4. In a small container with a lid, shake together the tomatoes, basil, garlic, vinegar and oil until well mixed.

Option 1: Salad

Arrange the peppers on fresh lettuce greens. Pour the dressing over the salad and serve topped with pine nuts.

Option 2: Pasta

Mix together the roasted peppers and the dressing. Add the crushed chilli flakes and salt. Toss with hot, freshly cooked pasta. Top with pine nuts.

Spaghetti Squash with Couscous Stuffing

This is a great dish to serve at Thanksgiving or at any other meal which traditionally has a turkey for meat-eaters.

1 cup couscous
1 ½ cups vegan "chicken flavour" stock
1 tsp salt
2 tbsp olive oil
½ cup raisins (optional)
2 tsp grated orange rind
4 tbsp orange juice
2 ½ cups pistachio nuts, coarsely chopped
½ cups fresh basil, chopped
1 large spaghetti squash, cut in half lengthways and seeds scrapped out

Easy Gravy (optional):
2 cups vegan "chicken flavour" stock (I use 2 stock cubes for a well-flavoured gravy)
1 tbsp corn starch mixed with 1 tbsp water
Salt if needed

Serves 4

1. Heat the oven to 400'F / 200'C / Gas Mark 6
2. Put the couscous in a bowl and pour in the **hot** stock. Cover and allow to sit for 5 minutes. Stir in the salt, oil, raisins, orange rind, orange juice, nuts and basil.
3. Carefully cut a small piece off the bottom of the squash so it can sit without wobbling. Stuff each half with the couscous.
4. Bake uncovered for 30 minutes then cover with foil and continue to cook for another hour or until the squash is very tender and a sharp knife can easily be inserted into the side.
5. **To make easy gravy**, bring the stock to a boil in a small pan. Stir in the corn starch and water, and keep stirring as it thickens. Serve immediately.

There is some debate about what the best temperature is for baking stuffed vegetables. Suggestions range from 350'F to 450'F, so I usually settle for the mid-point of 400'F. If you're baking other things at the same time, set the oven for whatever works best for your dinner. The squash will take longer to cook at a lower temperature, and make sure you cover it with foil to stop it from burning at higher temperatures.

Squash With Cranberry Stuffing

This dish goes nicely with nut roast and onion gravy.

¾ cup apple juice
½ cup dried cranberries
2 tbsp vegan margarine
1 onion, finely chopped
2 celery stalks, finely chopped
4 garlic cloves, finely chopped
1 tsp dried thyme
1 tsp dried oregano
1 tbsp dried parsley
¼ tsp cinnamon
2 cups of fresh breadcrumbs
¼ tsp black pepper
1 tsp salt
1 large squash such as Hubbard Squash or Acorn Squash, or a Pie Pumpkin
Serves 4

1. Heat the oven to 400'F / 200'C / Gas Mark 6
2. In a small bowl, mix together the apple juice and cranberries.
3. Heat the margarine in a large frying pan and cook the onion, celery and garlic over a high heat until soft but not browned, about 5 minutes. Add the thyme, oregano, parsley and cinnamon and cook for 1 minute.
4. Put the breadcrumbs in a large bowl and add the fried onion and celery along with the cranberries, apple juice, pepper and salt. Mix well.
5. Cut the top off the squash and scrape out the seeds. If necessary cut a small slice off the bottom of the squash so that it doesn't wobble. Put it on a baking tray and stuff with the breadcrumb mixture. Put the top back on.
6. Bake for 50 minutes to 1 hour or until a knife can easily be inserted into the sides of the soft squash. Check during baking and cover with foil if the stuffing is starting to get too brown. Allow to sit for 5 minutes before cutting into pieces and serving.

To make your own breadcrumbs for a gluten-free meal, try using quinoa bread. It seems to crumble better than other gluten-free breads.

Sweet Potatoes with Peanut Sauce

This is a taste of the tropics with sweet potatoes, pineapple juice and peanuts. If you don't like white cabbage try using finely sliced Napa cabbage or finely chopped carrots instead.

If you can find **crispy plantain chips** at your grocery store they make a lovely topping for this dish. If you can't locate any, try adding some finely chopped roasted peanuts instead. It's obviously not the same, but it will give you a bit of a crunch.

6 tbsp vegetable oil
1 large onion, finely chopped
4 garlic cloves, crushed
2 tbsp chopped fresh ginger
2 tsp paprika
½ tsp cayenne pepper
3 sweet potatoes, peeled and cubed
1 can (28 oz) diced tomatoes

1 cup pineapple juice
2 cups finely chopped white cabbage
½ cup crunchy peanut butter
1 tsp salt
1 tbsp lime juice
Crispy plantain chips (if available) to garnish

Serves 4

1. Heat the oil in a large saucepan and cook the onion over a medium heat until soft, about 5 minutes.
2. Add the garlic, ginger, paprika and cayenne and cook gently for 2 minutes. Add the sweet potatoes and mix well.
3. Add the tomatoes and pineapple juice. Cover and simmer over a low heat for about 30 minutes, or until the sweet potatoes are tender.
4. Stir in the cabbage, peanut butter, salt and lime juice. Cover and continue cooking for 10 minutes. Top with plantain chips and serve hot.

Tropical Sweet Potato Stew

I like to top this with 2 or 3 thinly sliced jalapeno chillies fried in 2 tbsp oil with 3 cloves of garlic and ½ tsp of paprika. I'm told it's not necessary to have chillies with every dish, but I've yet to be convinced that this is true.

4 tbsp vegetable oil
2 large onions, finely chopped
6 garlic cloves, crushed
2 tbsp finely chopped fresh ginger
1 tsp cinnamon
1 tsp dried crushed red chillies
1 tsp allspice
1 tsp ground black pepper
1 tsp turmeric

2 cups sweet potato, peeled and cubed
1 cup thinly sliced carrots
1 tsp dried thyme
1 cup fresh or 2 tbsp dried parsley
1 can / 2 cups coconut milk
2 tbsp tomato paste
1 tsp salt
2 cups thinly sliced kale or spinach
1 cup chopped roasted unsalted peanuts

Serves 4

1. Heat the oil in a deep pan. Add the onions, garlic and ginger and fry over a medium heat until the onion is soft, about 10 minutes.
2. Add the cinnamon, chillies, allspice, pepper and turmeric and cook for another 3 minutes or until fragrant. Add the sweet potato, carrots, thyme, parsley, coconut milk, tomato paste and salt. Bring to the boil, reduce the heat, cover and simmer gently for about 40 minutes or until the vegetables are tender.
3. Add the kale, cover and continue to simmer gently for 10 minutes.
4. Serve topped with the nuts.

Vegan Lasagne with Roasted Eggplant

This is a fabulous roasted vegetable lasagna which takes a bit of time to prepare but then quietly sits in the oven while you serve nibbles and drinks to your dinner guests. When you're ready to eat, whip it out and serve with a simple salad for easy casual entertaining.

Vegetable Layers:
1 large eggplant
1 large zucchini
2 red peppers
1 onion, cut into thick slices
2 tsp salt
Freshly ground black pepper

Tofu Layers: Make double if you like white sauces.
1 box (about 530g / 17 oz) soft tofu, drained
½ cup fresh parsley, chopped
1 tbsp lemon juice, plus more as needed (from about 1/2 lemon)
1 tsp salt
½ tsp ground black pepper
1 tbsp dried oregano

Tomato Sauce Layers: Make double if you like it saucy.
1 jar of pasta sauce (it's so much easier than making your own!)
2 tbsp capers (optional)

Pasta Layers:
180g / 7 oz oven ready lasagna (usually 6 pieces)

Serves 4

What happened to pasta sauce? Jars of pasta sauce used to be 1 liter, but now they're only 650ml. This makes me sad. But what makes me sadder is that some of them now contain fish oil. Who on earth would want fish oil in their tomato sauce? Check the ingredients before you put a jar in your shopping basket - you never know what might be in there!

1. Heat the oven to 400'F / 200'C / Gas Mark 6.
2. **To make the vegetable layer**: Put the eggplant, zucchini, peppers and onion on a foil-lined baking tray and sprinkle with salt and pepper. Bake for 45 minutes or until the peppers are charred and the eggplant is soft and shrivelled.
3. When the peppers are cool enough to handle, remove the skin and seeds. Slice the eggplant, zucchini and peppers.
4. **To make the herb sauce**: Put the tofu in a blender with the parsley, lemon juice, salt, pepper and oregano. Process until smooth.
5. **To make the tomato sauce**: Mix together the pasta sauce and capers.
6. **To assemble the lasagne**: Get a 9" x 13" baking pan and put the ingredients in as follows:

Layer 1 (Bottom): Tomato sauce (1/3 of the jar)
Layer 2: Pasta (usually 3 sheets)
Layer 3: Tofu sauce (1/2 of the sauce)
Layer 4: Eggplant and onion (all of it)
Layer 5: Tomato sauce (1/3 of the jar)
Layer 6: Pasta (usually 3 sheets)
Layer 7: Tofu sauce (the remaining half)
Layer 8: Red peppers and zucchini (all of them)
Layer 9: Pasta sauce (empty the jar)

5. Put the dish on a baking sheet to catch any spills and bake for 50 minutes or until hot and bubbling.

If you want, add some grated vegan cheese to the tofu sauce and sprinkle some over the top of the dish before baking. Cover with foil for the first 40 minutes to prevent the cheese from burning.

You can also make a traditional lasagna by replacing the roasted veggies with 450g / 1 lb veggie grounds fried with 2 tbsp oil, 1 onion and 2 garlic cloves. Mix with the tomato sauce and layer with pasta and tofu-vegan-cheese sauce.

Salads

I don't like salads with heavy dressings, and never buy pre-made ones in squeezy bottles. However, if you like them just make sure you read the ingredients and check for milk, cheese, fish or meaty bits. You might enjoy bacon bits in a Caesar salad, but it's not something a vegan would want to find sitting on their lettuce. Some quick and easy vegan salad dressings are:

Tahini and Lemon Dressing
½ cup tahini
½ cup apple cider vinegar
¼ cup soy sauce
1 tbsp lemon juice
½ tsp salt
4 garlic cloves, crushed
½ cup water
¼ cup fresh parsley
1 tbsp unrefined raw sugar
½ cup olive oil

Creamy Dressing
170g / 6 oz soft tofu, drained
2 tbsp lemon juice
1 tbsp olive oil
½ tsp salt
¼ tsp ground black pepper
2 tbsp fresh parsley, chopped
1 garlic clove, crushed
2 tsp cider vinegar

Put the ingredients for your chosen dressing in a blender and process until smooth.

Apple Salad

This pretty salad can be made using sweet apples such a Royal Gala (my favourite) or tart apples such as Granny Smiths, according to your personal tastes. I buy organic apples and leave the peel on for extra colour.

3 apples, washed, dried and very thinly sliced
3 cups of Napa cabbage, thinly sliced
1 ½ tbsp fresh lime juice
½ tsp salt
2 tbsp olive oil
1 medium red onion, finely chopped
1 jalapeno chilli, finely sliced
½ tsp turmeric
1 tbsp finely chopped fresh ginger

Serves 4

1. Mix together the apples, cabbage, lime juice and salt in a large bowl.
2. Heat the oil in a large frying pan. Add the onion and cook over a medium heat until soft, about 5 minutes.
3. Add the chilli, turmeric and ginger. Cook for another minute then stir into the apple and cabbage.
4. Chill for 30 minutes before serving.

Avocado and Grapefruit Salad

I like to make this with walnut oil for a hint of nuttiness (keep it in the fridge once it has been opened) but extra virgin olive oil will also work well.

Mache, also known as lamb's lettuce, has a slightly nutty taste which goes well with this salad. If it's not available just use whatever baby salad leaves you can get your hands on.

½ cup grapefruit or orange juice (save the juice when you chop up the grapefruit)
1 tsp fresh ginger, grated
2 tbsp walnut or olive oil
1 tbsp lemon juice
2 tbsp balsamic vinegar
1 tbsp unrefined raw sugar
2 avocado, peeled and cubed
3 grapefruit, peeled and segmented. Toss with a bit of sugar if it's *really* sour!
4 - 6 cups Mache, baby spinach or arugula
Freshly ground black pepper

Serves 4

1. In a small container with a lid, shake together the grapefruit juice, ginger, walnut oil, lemon juice, vinegar and sugar.
2. Toss the avocado with the grapefruit segments and arrange on a plate on top of the salad leaves.
3. Pour a small amount of dressing over the salad and serve the remainder in a jug on the side. Grind a little black pepper on top of the salad and serve immediately.

Celery, Oyster Mushroom and Grape Salad

I like to use praline pecans (made without dairy products) in the salad when I can find them at my local store, but natural pecans (or whatever nuts you fancy) work just fine too.

King oyster mushrooms can be quite expensive, so feel free to make this salad with a mixture of different mushrooms to make it more economical, or, if you like the leafy green stuff, halve the quantity of mushrooms and mix in 4 cups of salad greens just before serving.

500g /1 lb king oyster mushrooms, sliced
¼ cup olive oil
1 tsp salt
2 cups seedless grapes, cut in half
1 ½ cups celery, sliced thinly
2 tbsp finely chopped Italian parsley
½ cup finely chopped praline pecans

Dressing:
1 garlic clove, finely chopped
1 ½ tbsp sesame oil
2 cups flat-leaf parsley, coarsely chopped
½ tsp salt

Serves 4

1. Toss the mushrooms with the olive oil and salt. Put in a frying pan and cook until very lightly browned. Set aside.
2. Mix together the grapes, celery and parsley. Stir in the nuts and cooked mushrooms.
3. **To make the dressing**: Mix together the garlic and sesame oil. Add the parsley and salt to taste. If you have a food processor, feel free to turn it into a chunky paste. I don't bother.
4. Add the dressing to the mushroom mixture and mix gently.

Cucumber, Nectarine and Orange Salad

I freely admit that I made this salad with nectarines in it because I only had one orange on hand at the time. I really needed 3 oranges, so I made the best out of what was available, and it tasted great.

Orange flower water, also known as orange blossom water, is available in many supermarkets and Middle Eastern grocery stores. Try stirring a tablespoon into couscous before cooking it.

1 orange, peeled and coarsely chopped
2 nectarines (or another 2 oranges), unpeeled, coarsely chopped
½ English cucumber, soft middle removed, peeled and coarsely chopped
1 tbsp lemon juice
2 tsp sugar
1 tbsp orange flower water (optional, but really nice)
½ tsp cinnamon
Pinch of salt
1 tbsp finely chopped fresh mint

Serves 4

1. Mix everything together in a pretty bowl.
2. Chill for at least 15 minutes before serving.

Eggplant and Chickpea Salad with Red Pepper Salsa

Before the invention of microwave ovens, eggplants were usually cooked in oil until soft and somewhat greasy. I usually pierce the eggplant skin in multiple locations (to stop it from exploding) and pop it into the microwave on full power for about 5 minutes or until soft. Other people swear steaming eggplants is the way to go, or they can be baked in the oven for about 45 minutes. Or, if you like, you can chop it into bite sized pieces and stir-fry it in lots of oil.

Eggplant Salad:
1 large eggplant, cooked and cut into bite-sized pieces
1 can / 2 cups cooked chickpeas, rinsed
4 tbsp olive oil
½ tsp salt (or more to taste)
2 garlic cloves, crushed
1 tsp lemon juice
½ tsp hot sauce (or to taste)
½ cup chopped fresh coriander

Salsa:
2 garlic cloves, finely chopped
1 sweet onion, finely chopped
½ green pepper, finely chopped
½ red pepper, finely chopped
1 jalapeno chilli, finely chopped
1 large fresh tomato, finely chopped
½ tsp salt

Serves 4

1. Mix together all the ingredients for the salsa.
2. In a separate dish, mix together all the ingredients for the salad. It is best served while the eggplant is still warm.

Mango and Orange Salad

This is a very simple side dish to go with just about any curry and a multitude of other dishes. If you want it to be fairly mild, remove the seeds from the chilli.

2 sweet oranges, peeled and coarsely chopped
2 ripe mangos, coarsely chopped
½ cup white onion, finely chopped
1 jalapeno chilli, finely chopped
2 tbsp fresh coriander, chopped
Salt and pepper to taste

Serves 4

Mix all the ingredients together and allow to sit for 30 minutes before serving.

Orange, Napa Cabbage and Peanut Salad

I found the inspiration for this salad in, of all places, an African cookbook. I have changed it somewhat from the original recipe, most notably by taking out the sardines. I'm not talking about freshly cooked sardines either - the recipe called for a can of sardines. It sounded totally revolting. Here is a much-improved fish-free version!

½ cup roasted, unsalted peanuts, chopped
1 small Napa cabbage (about 6 cups)
1 orange, peeled and chopped
5 green onions, thinly sliced

Dressing:
1 tbsp grated fresh ginger
Juice of 2 limes
1 garlic clove, crushed
1 jalapeno chilli, deseeded and finely chopped
¼ cup soy sauce
¼ cup olive oil
1 ½ tsp sesame oil
1 tbsp peanut butter
2 tbsp toasted sesame seeds

Serves 4

1. In a large bowl, mix together the peanuts, cabbage, orange and green onions.
2. In a container with a lid, mix together the ginger, lime juice, garlic, chilli, soy sauce, olive oil, sesame oil and peanut butter. Use the back of a spoon to squish the peanut butter into the other ingredients. Put the lid on and shake vigorously until well mixed.
3. Just before serving, toss the salad in the dressing and top with sesame seeds.

Orange and Walnut Salad

So simple, yet so tasty.

6 cups baby spinach
1 orange, peeled and cut into chunks (grate the rind before peeling the orange - you will need it later!)
1 cup toasted walnuts

Dressing:
¼ cup olive oil
1 tbsp balsamic vinegar
1 tsp Dijon mustard
¼ tsp salt
1 garlic cloves, crushed
1 tbsp orange juice
1 tsp grated orange rind

Serves 4

1. Toss together the spinach, orange, walnuts and baby spinach.
2. In a jar with a lid, shake together the olive oil, vinegar, mustard, salt, garlic, orange juice and rind. Pour over the salad and serve immediately.

Strawberry Quinoa Salad

I was quietly eating quinoa back in the 80's, unaware that in the then-distant future it would gain a reputation as being a "super food". I'm beginning to suspect that we hippy vegetarians of the 80's weren't quite as crazy as our friends made us out to be!

2 cups cooked quinoa
2 tbsp olive oil
Juice and grated rind from 2 limes
1 tsp sugar
1 tsp salt
¼ cup fresh mint, chopped
¼ cup fresh parsley, chopped
¼ cups fresh basil chopped
1 cup sliced fresh strawberries
2 green onions, finely chopped

Optional extras: ½ cup fresh blueberries or ½ cup chopped toasted almonds

Serves 4

1. Mix together the cooked quinoa, olive oil, lime juice and rind, sugar and salt.
2. Fold in the mint, parsley, basil, strawberries and green onions. Add any of the options. Serve warm or at room temperature.

A Few Words About Grains

Cooking Rice

I have a confession to make: I have a rice cooker, and I couldn't live without it. We eat rice most days, and I really can't be bothered with trying to cook it on the stove. If you don't have a rice cooker, wash your rice well then add 1 cup of rice to 2 cups of **boiling** water (scale up depending on the number of people). Cover and simmer (don't remove the lid!) for 18 - 25 minutes. Start checking at 18 minutes - the rice should be tender with no crunchy bits.

I like to use **basmati** rice when serving curries and either short grain **calrose** rice or long grain **jasmine** rice when making oriental dishes. I'm not a fan of brown rice, figuring I get enough fiber from my diet of beans, lentils and vegetables. If you like the nutty taste and texture, check the packet for instructions on how to cook it. Different types of brown rice require different amounts of water and have different cooking times.

Cooking Quinoa

Quinoa (pronounced keenwa) is a fabulous grain filled with protein and has the bonus of being gluten-free. Rinse well before using. I cook mine in a rice cooker using a ratio of 2 cups of boiling water or vegan "chicken flavour" stock for 1 cup of washed, drained quinoa. Alternatively, you can gently simmer it in a pan covered with a lid until all the water has been absorbed. It takes about 20 minutes. Fluff using a fork, re-cover and allow to sit for a couple of minutes before serving.

Cooking Couscous

Couscous is a dried form of durum wheat. Corn based couscous is becoming increasingly available, which is usually gluten free. It's very easy to cook. Simply pour 1 ½ cups of boiling stock or water over 1 cup of couscous, cover and allow to sit for 5 minutes. Uncover and fluff with a fork before serving.

Hot Side Dishes

Most vegetables dishes are automatically vegan without changing any of the ingredients, as long as they're not fried in butter, covered in a cheese sauce or topped with crispy bacon! There's nothing wrong with serving simple steamed or stir fried broccoli with dinner, or a few cobs of fresh corn, or a pile of fresh peas. Bring on those veggies! I like the idea of getting my veggies from the local farmer's market, but ours is only there on Saturdays, and only during the no-snow months. I still try to shop seasonally when I can, even though supermarkets now offer just about everything year round. Locally grown veggies are good if you can get them, but sometimes you just have to take what you can find!

A lot of dishes which meat eaters would consider to be side dishes can actually become the main dish for a vegan if you add some tofu or nuts. This comes in especially handy at big family meals such as thanksgiving, which can be a pretty miserable occasion for a vegan in a non-vegan household, especially if there are turkey juices in the gravy and the potatoes are mixed with butter. If you have a vegan joining you, ask them if they want to bring their own protein dish such as a **tofurky** (I'm not a fan - I'm sure if you drop them they bounce) or some **tofu cutlets**. Alternatively, try making a nut roast or stuffed squash. You could also throw together some sprouts with veggie bacon, or maybe wrap some asparagus in filo pastry for a special side dish. Follow it up with a vegan pumpkin pie and I'm sure everyone will be happy.

Sometimes a jug of **vegan gravy** can make all the difference to a meat-free Thanksgiving dinner. Bisto instant beef gravy granules are currently vegan, but always read the ingredients to make sure they haven't changed since I wrote this.

Asparagus in Filo Pastry

This crispy, garlicky dish makes a great side dish or can be served as an appetizer. Don't overcook - soggy asparagus is nowhere near as nice as when it's hot and slightly crisp.

24 asparagus spears
12 sheets of filo pastry (you'll find it in the freezer section of your local grocery store)
¼ cup vegan margarine
4 garlic cloves, finely chopped
½ cup fresh parsley, finely chopped
Lemon slices to squeeze

Serves 4

1. Heat the oven to 375'F / 190°C /Gas Mark 5.
2. Bend each stem of asparagus near the base until it snaps and throw away the thick end.
3. Melt the margarine and mix in the garlic and parsley.
4. Cut the sheets of filo in half. Brush each sheet with garlic margarine and fold it in half.
5. Use the sheet to wrap two pieces of asparagus and cut them apart. Continue until all the asparagus has been wrapped. If you run out of margarine, just melt some more.

6. Place on a baking tray and bake for 15 -20 minutes until golden and crisp. Cool for 5 minutes before serving.

Asparagus with Lemon Grass

When it is in season, asparagus stalks are not too thick and have only a small amount of wasted woody stem. To determine where the woody part ends, gently bend an asparagus spear. It should, in theory, snap off where the tender part of the stem begins.

3 tbsp vegetable oil
3 garlic cloves, finely chopped
1 tbsp grated fresh ginger
2 jalapeno chillies, finely chopped
1 lemon grass stalk, finely sliced with dry outer layer removed, or 1 tsp grated lemon rind
2 handfuls trimmed asparagus spears
2 tbsp soy sauce
1 tsp sugar
3 tbsp unsalted roasted peanuts, finely chopped
¼ cup finely chopped fresh coriander

Serves 4

1. Heat the oil in a large frying pan. Add the garlic, ginger, chillies and lemon grass. Cook over a medium heat for 2 -3 minutes or until they are golden brown.
2. Add the asparagus and stir for another 2 minutes until it is tender but not soft.
3. Stir in the soy sauce and sugar. Mix well.
4. Add the peanuts and coriander then serve immediately.

Brussel Sprouts with Vegan "Bacon"

Vegan "bacon" adds a nice twist to good old brussel sprouts. I know when people say they don't like sprouts the usual response is "but you'll love this recipe", but if you don't like them you won't like this. It *is* brussel sprouts and it *tastes* like brussel sprouts. Personally, I love them when they're hot and still slightly crisp, but if they're over cooked and soggy there's no way I'm going to eat them!

If you can't find any veggie bacon (brands include Yves and Paradis) add ½ tsp of paprika instead.

6 cups of brussel sprouts, old or dirty outer leaves removed
3 tbsp olive oil
6 slices veggie bacon, coarsely chopped
4 garlic cloves, coarsely chopped
½ cup vegan "chicken flavour" stock
½ tsp salt
¼ tsp black pepper
2 tsp vegan margarine

Serves 4

1. Cut an 'X' in the core end of each sprout to help them cook evenly.
2. Heat the oil in a large pan and cook the "bacon" and garlic over a medium-high heat for about 5 minutes.
3. Add the sprouts, stock, salt and pepper. Bring to the boil then reduce the heat, cover and simmer gently until the sprouts are tender, 12 to 15 minutes. Do not overcook!
4. Stir in the remaining margarine and mix well. Serve immediately.

Cabbage with Spices

I like to buy bags of pre-chopped coleslaw rather than buying an actual cabbage and chopping it up. Sometimes it contains red cabbage, sometimes it contains carrots, and sometimes it contains nothing except white cabbage. Either way, I'm happy.

If you want it hotter, add a sliced jalapeno chilli along with the onions.

3 tbsp vegetable oil
1 tsp fennel seeds
1 tsp cumin seeds
1 tsp mustard seeds
1 large onion, coarsely chopped
½ tsp dried red chilli flakes
1 tbsp fresh ginger, grated
4 cups shredded cabbage
1 tsp salt

Serves 4

1. Heat the oil in a large frying pan then add the fennel, cumin and mustard seeds. Fry for 1 minute then add the onion, chillies and ginger. Fry over a medium heat until the onion is soft - about 5 minutes.
2. Add the cabbage and stir well. Cook over a medium heat for about 10 minutes or until the cabbage is slightly softened. Stir in the salt and serve immediately.

Cauliflower Roasted with Paprika

Paprika (smoked if you've got it!) gives cauliflower a lovely colour and a subtle boost of flavour when roasted in the oven. Don't overcook it. Soggy cauliflower is utterly foul!

3 tbsp olive oil
1 tsp paprika
½ tsp salt
1 garlic clove, crushed
1 jalapeno chilli, finely chopped
1 large cauliflower, broken into florets

Serves 4

1. Heat the oven to 400'F / 200'C / Gas Mark 6
2. Toss together the oil, paprika, salt, garlic, chilli and cauliflower. Put on a baking sheet.
3. Bake for 30 minutes until tender-crisp and lightly golden. Serve immediately.

Cashew Nut Rice

This is a great side dish with just about any Chinese entree but also makes a nice meal on its own if you are feeling lazy. I always cook this in my trusty rice cooker.

2 tbsp vegetable oil
1 tbsp vegan margarine
1 onion, finely chopped
½ red pepper, finely chopped
½ orange pepper, finely chopped
1 carrot, grated
2 tbsp sesame seeds
1 ½ cups Chinese long grain rice
5 tbsp white wine
3 cups "chicken flavour" stock
2 tsp soy sauce
1 cup unsalted cashew nuts
4 green onions, finely chopped

Serves 4

1. Heat the oil and the margarine in a frying pan. Add the onion, peppers, carrot and sesame seeds. Cook over a medium heat for 10 minutes or until the onion is soft and lightly golden.
2. Transfer to your rice cooker, stir in the rice, wine, stock and soy sauce. Pop on the lid, press the "cook" button and leave it to do its job. Alternatively, add the rice, stock and soy sauce to the ingredients in the pan, bring to a boil, cover tightly and simmer very gently for 18 - 20 minutes or until all the liquid has been absorbed and the rice is cooked.
3. Stir in the cashew nuts and green onions and serve immediately.

Cornmeal Fried Rice

The seasonings can be varied according to your mood. Try just plain salt and pepper, or premixed BBQ spices, or maybe some mixed dried herbs. Sprinkle with salt and serve with something to dip the squares in such as a chilli, stew or curry.

2 - 3 cups freshly cooked rice, preferably short grain such as calrose
½ cup cornmeal
1 tsp salt
½ tsp crushed dried red chillies
1 tsp dried oregano
1 tsp paprika
1 cup vegetable oil

Serves 4

1. Squash the warm rice into a plastic box - I use a rectangular lunch-sized box about 4" x 8". Cover with plastic wrap and allow to cool.
2. Mix together the cornmeal, salt, chillies, oregano and paprika.
3. Tip the squashed rice out the box and cut into 1" squares. If you squished it hard enough it should stick together. Coat the squares in the seasoned cornmeal.
4. Heat the oil in a large frying pan. When hot, cook the squares until every side is golden brown. I find medium-high heat works best so that they don't burn. It takes 2 - 3 minutes per side. You may have to do this in batches. When cooked, transfer to a kitchen paper covered plate and allow to cool slightly. Serve warm with a chilli or other saucy dinner.

If you make these ahead of time, reheat them in a 350'F / 180'C / Gas Mark 4 oven for 20 minutes.

Garlic Green Beans

These don't look very exciting but they taste great. You can either cook them in a frying pan or pop them in a hot oven (400'F/ 200'C / Gas Mark 6) for 15 - 20 minutes.

4 tbsp sesame oil
4 cups fresh green beans, trimmed
10 garlic cloves, finely chopped
½ tsp salt
½ tsp crushed dried red chillies

Serves 4

1. Heat the oil in a frying pan and cook the beans over a high heat for 5 minutes or until starting to brown.
2. Add the garlic, salt and chillies and cook for 2 more minutes. Serve immediately.

Garlic Mushrooms

This is really good as a side dish or as an appetizer served with crusty dairy-free bread.

2 tbsp olive oil or vegan margarine
450g / 1 lb white or coffee mushrooms, cut in half if large
4 garlic cloves, finely chopped
2 tsp lemon juice
¼ cup chopped flat-leaf parsley
2 tsp salt or to taste (it should be nicely salty)

Serves 4

1. Heat the oil in a large frying pan. Cook the mushrooms and garlic over a medium-high heat for 10 minutes or until soft.
2. Stir in the lemon juice and parsley and add salt to taste. Serve immediately.

Panko Potatoes

These oven-baked crispy potato balls go really well with everything from an Indian curry to a nut roast. Soft on the inside, crunchy on the outside, and very easy to make. They're also a really nice way to use up left-over mashed potatoes.

Panko is flaky dried breadcrumbs often used in Japanese cooking. I find it in my local grocery store, but it's also available at Asian supermarkets. In the unlikely event that you can't find any, use a packet of dried breadcrumbs (rice breadcrumbs are usually gluten free). It will be different to the panko potatoes but quite yummy anyway.

4 medium size potatoes, peeled and cut into 4 pieces
Large pan of water
2 tbsp vegan margarine
1 tsp salt
1 cup Japanese panko flakes

Serves 4

1. Heat the oven to 400'F / 200'C / Gas Mark 6
2. Put the potatoes into a large pan of water and bring to the boil. Reduce the heat, cover and simmer for 20 minutes or until the potatoes are soft.
3. Drain the potatoes and return to the pan. Mash with the margarine and salt. I don't know if it's because of my British upbringing, but I like mine lumpy.
4. When cool enough to handle, mold the potato into small balls and roll in the panko flakes. Place on a baking sheet.
5. Put in the oven for 30 - 35 minutes or until golden brown.

Roasted Kale

This side dish couldn't be easier. If you don't like kale try another leafy green vegetable instead.

2 bunches kale, thick stems and ribs removed, leaves coarsely chopped
2 tbsp extra-virgin olive oil
2 pinches of salt
½ a lime to squeeze (optional)

Serves 4

1. Preheat the oven to 375'F / 190'C / Gas Mark 5.
2. In a large bowl or clean plastic hole-free grocery bag, toss the kale with the olive oil and the salt. Spread out the kale on a large baking sheet or two.
3. Bake for about 20 minutes or until crispy at the edges but not turned into charcoal.
4. Squeeze lime juice on the hot kale if desired and serve immediately.

I don't know what all the fuss is over crispy kale, but it currently seems to be the "in" food which everyone is raving about. My mom was way ahead of her time when she tried to feed crispy cabbage stuff to me and my siblings back in the 70's. At the time we most definitely were NOT impressed!

Roast Potatoes

This goes nicely with just about any main dish.

4 - 6 medium potatoes, scrubbed
Spray oil or 4 tbsp olive oil
Salt to sprinkle

Serves 4

1. Heat the oven to 425'F / 220'C / Gas Mark 7
2. Trim a small amount off the bottom of the potatoes so they will sit in the pan without wobbling.
3. Make sideways cuts in the potatoes which are close together and do not go all the way down to the bottom.
4. Spray or brush with oil and sprinkle with salt. Bake for 45 minutes to 1 hour or until soft and golden brown.

Roast Potato Wedges

If you have a pre-mixed BBQ seasoning lying around, try putting that on the potatoes.

4 -6 medium potatoes, scrubbed and cut into wedges
2 tbsp olive oil
1 tsp paprika
1 tsp oregano
1 tsp salt

Serves 4

1. Heat the oven to 400'F / 200'C / Gas Mark 6
2. Mix the potato wedges with the oil, paprika, oregano and salt.
3. Put on a baking sheet and bake for 40 -50 minutes or until soft and golden brown.

118

Root Vegetable Mash

I'm not a fan of plain old mashed potatoes, even if they're pepped up with roasted garlic or herbs. This dish adds a bit more interest to a dinner plate - root vegetable mash. The quantities here are just suggestions - change the recipe according to whatever you have lurking in your kitchen. Try adding different herbs such as a tablespoon of finely chopped fresh rosemary, or if you like things spicy, stir in some chilli pepper flakes.

2 medium potatoes, peeled and cut into 4 pieces
2 medium sweet potatoes, peeled and cut into 4 pieces
1 medium carrot, peeled and thinly sliced
2 parsnips, peeled and thinly sliced
1 garlic clove, crushed
2 tbsp dried parsley
3 cups vegan "chicken" or vegetable stock
2 tbsp vegan margarine
1 tsp salt
1 tsp ground black pepper

Serves 4

1. Put all the vegetables and parsley into a medium saucepan and add just enough stock to cover. Bring to the boil, pop the lid on, reduce the heat and simmer for 30 minutes. You want the vegetables to be soft.
2. Drain most of the stock out of the pan, leaving about 1 cup with the vegetables. Get a fork (or potato masher) and coarsely mash the veggies. You want them to be chunky.
3. Stir in the margarine, adding more or less according to your tastes. Check the seasoning and add salt if necessary. Stir in the black pepper and serve hot.

Sweet Potato Cakes

These can be cooked in batches and kept warm in the oven, or served at room temperature.

Sweet Potato Cakes:
3 or 4 large sweet potatoes
¾ cup flour
1 tsp salt
½ tsp sugar
3 tbsp chopped green onions
1 tsp crushed dried red chilli
2 tbsp dried parsley
3 tbsp olive oil
Lemon to squeeze

Salted Limes:
2 limes
½ tsp salt
1 tbsp olive oil

Serves 4

1. **To make the salted limes:** Remove the rind from the limes and cut the flesh into thin slices. Place in a small bowl, sprinkle with salt and mix in the olive oil.
2. **To make the sweet potato cakes**: Cook the sweet potatoes in the microwave until completely soft - about 8 minutes in my microwave oven. Alternatively, bake them for about 40 minutes at 350'F / 180'C / Gas Mark 4.
3. Allow the sweet potatoes to cool then peel off the skin. Mash with a fork or potato masher.
4. Mix together the sweet potatoes, flour, salt, sugar, green onions, chilli and parsley. Add more flour if needed to make a soft dough.
5. Heat the oil in a large frying pan. Add a tablespoon of dough and squash it with a spatula until it is about ½" thick. Add more pancakes but make sure you leave enough room to easily turn them over. Cook over a medium heat for about 6 minutes per side. Serve hot or at room temperature with the salted limes.

Vegan Barbeques

One of the strangest food-related things I think anyone has ever said to me is "We were planning on inviting you round on Saturday, but I'm afraid we're having a barbeque so..." What? There seems to be a fairly common misconception that vegans and barbeques are incompatible. Well let me tell you, that simply isn't true. There are many vegan-friendly barbeque options (I'm beginning to think some people have never heard of **vegetables**). Besides vegetables and **tofu**, there are now many readily available **vegan burgers**, **vegan hot dogs, vegan "chicken breasts"** and even **vegan sausages** which can be thrown on the barbie. Serve them on an organic bun (check your local grocery store and natural food store for vegan options) with grilled veggies and a salad, and poof... there's a vegan barbeque.

Faux chicken breasts are great on the grill and can be brushed with a marinade if you like. Make sure you oil the grill well as they, like many vegan options, tend to stick. I'm also rather fond of Lick's brand veggie burgers which, unlike some of the thin alternatives, don't taste like cardboard. Don't go through the hassle of trying to make your own veggie burgers from scratch - it's really not worth the effort. Veggie hot dogs (I like the Yves brand) can be found in most grocery stores and are easy to throw on the BBQ. Don't overcook them unless you want them to be somewhat rubbery. I've also had some nice meals made with vegan sausages.

Please don't let bits of meat from your grill get stuck on the bottom of vegan food. People who don't eat animals really don't appreciate a bit of cow stuck on their veggies. Try cooking vegan foods on a piece of oiled foil or on a throw-away grilling tray. True, they won't get grill-lines, but they also won't get "meated".

A Few Words About Veggies on the Grill

Just about any vegetable can be cooked over a flame, making it possible to have a wide, varied assortment of dishes at a BBQ which can be enjoyed by vegans and non-vegans alike. If you want to pep things up a little, make some herb or spice "butter" to go with the veggies, made using vegan margarine. I like the Earth Balance brand. Feel free to make up your own recipes, but these are three of my favourites. Simply mix the ingredients together and pop in the fridge for half an hour before putting on top of freshly grilled veggies or potatoes.

Lime "Butter"

½ cup vegan margarine, room temperature
Grated rind of 1 lime
1 ½ tsp lime juice
½ tsp ground black pepper
½ garlic clove, crushed
1 tbsp finely chopped fresh parsley
¼ tsp dried red crushed chilli
Salt to taste

Garlic "Butter"

½ cup vegan margarine, room temperature
3 garlic cloves, crushed
¼ cup finely chopped fresh parsley
Salt to taste

Tarragon "Butter"

½ cup vegan margarine, room temperature
3 tbsp finely chopped fresh tarragon
1 tsp grated orange rind
2 tsp finely chopped fresh chives
Small garlic clove, crushed (optional)
Salt to taste

Barbequed Potato Packets

The potatoes for this dish are wrapped in foil and steamed on the barbeque rather than being cooked directly on the grill. This is a great way to make sure bits of steak stuck on the grill don't end up on the bottom of a vegan potato side dish! If you're cooking a large number of potatoes, either increase the cooking time or divide the potatoes between two packets.

Try cooking butternut squash, pumpkin or sweet potatoes this way. You could also try carrots, but increase the cooking time if you want them soft.

4 medium potatoes, scrubbed and cut into thin slices
3 tbsp olive oil
1 tsp salt
3 garlic cloves, crushed
1 tsp dried oregano
½ lemon, cut into 4 slices
2 tbsp water

Serves 4

1. Mix together the potatoes, olive oil, salt, garlic, oregano, and lemon.
2. Place on a piece of foil large enough to make into a sealed pouch. Add 2 tablespoons of water and fold up the pouch.
3. Cook over a direct medium heat for 20 - 25 minutes or until the potatoes are tender. Serve hot.

Barbequed Bok Choy

Putting bok choy on the BBQ creates a fabulously crunchy side dish. Yes, some of the thin leaves will turn into charcoal but that's part of the fun when cooking things on the grill. You can do this for just about any leafy green vegetable with delicious results.

Large bag (about 900g / 2 lb) baby bok choy
¼ cup vegan margarine
2 garlic cloves, crushed

Serves 4

1. Cook the bok choy over direct medium heat for 6 - 8 minutes, turning once.
2. Put the margarine and garlic in a microwavable dish and cook until the margarine is melted - about 30 seconds.
3. Transfer the cooked bok choy to a dish and pour the garlic margarine over the top. Serve at once.

Grilled Cauliflower Salad

When I was younger, I really didn't like raw cauliflower because it seemed to squeak on my teeth. The cauliflower in this salad is wrapped in foil and partially cooked on the BBQ so that it's still tender but hot and doesn't squeak! You can also try this with **broccoli**.

1 tsp turmeric
2 tsp water
1 medium cauliflower, broken into florets
2 medium tomatoes, cut into 8 pieces
1 large onion, thinly sliced
½ cup black or green olives

4 tbsp olive oil
½ tsp dried oregano
½ tsp dried basil
Salt and pepper to taste
1 tbsp water
¼ cup chopped fresh parsley

Serves 4

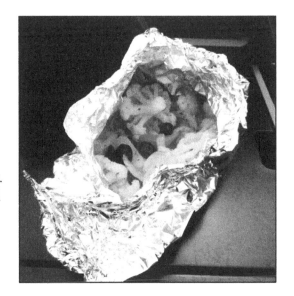

1. Mix the turmeric with the water.
2. Toss the cauliflower with the turmeric. Add the tomatoes, onion, olives, olive oil, oregano, basil, salt and pepper.
3. Place on a piece of foil large enough to make into a sealed pouch. Add a tablespoon of water and fold up the pouch. Cook over a direct medium heat for 15 - 20 minutes or until the cauliflower is tender but not soggy.
4. Carefully tip the contents of the foil into a large bowl and mix in the parsley. Add more salt if needed and serve warm or at room temperature.

There was a phase in my life when I couldn't eat cooked cauliflower after my parents' vegetable patch was invaded by caterpillars. No matter how many my mom picked out, there were always some boiled caterpillars floating in the pan at dinner time. That image stayed with me for a long time. I like my cauliflower to be vegan!

Grilled Eggplant with Peanut Sauce

I just love, love, love grilled eggplants. Their soft flesh and chewy skin combined with the subtle smokiness of the flames make it worth standing under the blazing sun to cook them.

Try variations of this sauce using **almond** or **cashew butter**, or replace the dried red chilli with a finely chopped **fresh jalapeno pepper**.

2 large eggplants, cut into ½" thick slices
4 tbsp vegetable oil
2 garlic cloves, crushed

Serves 4

1. Mix together the oil and crushed garlic. Brush onto the eggplant and grill over a direct medium heat for 8 - 10 minutes, turning once.

Dressing:
2 tbsp grated ginger
5 garlic cloves, crushed
½ tsp dried crushed red chilli flakes
¼ cup peanut butter
3 tbsp soy sauce
1 tsp sesame oil
1 ½ tbsp unrefined raw sugar
2 tbsp water
2 green onions, finely chopped

1. Mix the ginger, garlic, chillies, peanut butter, soy sauce, sesame oil, sugar and water together until well combined.
2. Spoon a small amount of the dressing over the eggplant and serve the remainder in a small dish. Top the eggplant with green onions and serve at room temperature.

Herbed Tofu and Vegetable Kebabs

This makes an easy and attractive change from barbequed veggie burgers and veggie dogs.

6 cups bite size vegetables such as chopped zucchini, mushrooms, broccoli, cauliflower and cherry tomatoes
450g / 16 oz firm tofu, cubed
¼ cup olive oil
2 tbsp dried mixed herbs such as parsley, oregano, basil and thyme
1 tsp salt
Wood skewers (soaked in water) or metal BBQ skewers

Serves 4

1. Mix together the vegetables, tofu, oil, herbs and salt. Leave for about an hour.
2. Carefully put the vegetables and tofu on the skewers then cook over a direct heat for 10 - 15 minutes or until browned.

A Few Words About Sugar

What's all the fuss about white sugar?

Many, but not all, vegans eat standard white processed sugar. It makes life easier when eating out or buying baked goods. However, when maintaining a cruelty-free lifestyle this isn't ideal. Cane sugar is processed using activated charcoal, which may be made from animal bones. It is impossible to tell from a package of sugar if it was processed with animal or plant based charcoal. Brown sugar is usually processed white sugar with molasses added to it.

An easy way around the charcoal problem is to use unprocessed raw sugar, which is now readily available at many large chain grocery stores and in natural food stores. I like to buy fair trade organic unprocessed sugar. Yes, it costs more than standard white sugar, but I use so little of it in a year that it really doesn't make a difference to my food costs. I also think it tastes better than refined sugar. If I need powdered sugar I just buy whatever I can get. At the time of writing, Redpath sugar is vegan.

Why don't most vegans eat honey?

Honey can be a bit of a contentious issue for vegans. A minority eat honey from organic, small-scale bee keepers, while others avoid it completely as it involves exploitation of animals. Vegans generally replace honey with other sweeteners such as organic maple syrup, raw sugar or agave syrup, which comes from the agave plant found in central Mexico.

Do Vegans Eat Maple Syrup?

Maple syrup is a natural product extracted from maple trees and then boiled down to form a syrup. In the past, most commercial maple syrup manufacturers used lard as an anti-foaming agent, which rendered the maple syrup non-vegan. These days vegetable oil is commonly used instead. Any maple syrup labelled as "kosher" will not have been processed using lard, and this is also the case for most organic brands.

Sweet Treats

There are a lot of vegan-friendly desserts which can be made with very little effort. A few examples are:

- **Fresh fruit** cooked gently with a little **maple syrup** and served over **vegan ice cream** (you'll find some in your local store, usually made with soy or coconut).
- **Bananas** microwaved, fried or oven baked with a small amount of vegan **margarine**, a touch of **allspice or cinnamon** and some unrefined raw **sugar**.
- **Peaches** cut in half and popped on the **BBQ** until warm and slightly caramelised.
- **Apples** cored and stuffed with a mixture of **dried fruit**, unrefined raw **sugar** and **cinnamon**. Wrap in foil and bake or cook on the BBQ until soft.
- Chilled sliced **honeydew melon** sprinkled with a pinch of dried **ginger** (my grandad's favourite) topped with a glace cherry on a stick.
- **Strawberries** dipped in dairy-free dark **chocolate** and allowed to set.
- Make a **pie** using store-bought pastry (check the ingredients) and the fruit of your choice.
- Check your local grocery store for vegan **cookies** - at the time of writing Oreos are vegan!
- Make a **fruit cobbler**, crumble or crisp using vegan margarine.

If you want to convert your regular sweet treat recipes into a vegan delights, you can swap the milk with a non-dairy replacement such as soy or almond milk. Butter can be replaced with non-dairy margarine, and unrefined raw sugar can take the place of white or brown sugar. Organic maple syrup is a good stand-in for honey.

Useful Egg Replacements for ONE egg:
¼ **cup soft tofu, or**
1 small banana or ½ an avocado, mashed, or
¼ **cup applesauce, or**
2 tbsp corn starch or
Vegan powdered egg replacements

Banana Coconut "Ice Cream" Pie

I have a hearty dislike of traditional banana cream pie. I only tried it once and it caused all kinds of unpleasant gastric excitement. This vegan version, however, agrees with both my taste buds and my digestive tract, which is a great relief to the people I live with.

Shake the can of coconut milk vigorously before opening to mix the contents together.

Base:
14 digestive biscuits, crushed in a plastic bag with a rolling pin (about 2 cups)
½ cup vegan margarine, melted

Topping:
1 cup dark dairy-free chocolate chips
1 cup full-fat coconut milk
½ tsp pure vanilla extract

Filling:
¼ cup corn starch
¾ cup organic maple syrup
1 cup full-fat coconut milk
1 tbsp vegetable oil or virgin coconut oil
2 boxes silken tofu, 300g / 12oz each
2 large ripe bananas, mashed
½ tsp salt
½ tsp pure vanilla extract

Makes 10 mini desserts

1. Mix the crushed cookies with the melted margarine and press into the bottom of 8 jumbo muffin cups.
2. To make the filling, put the corn starch in a small pan and add the maple syrup and coconut milk, stirring constantly. Turn on the heat and continue to stir until the mixture boils. Turn the heat down and continue to stir for about 2 minutes or until it thickens slightly. Stir in the oil and transfer to a blender.
3. Add the tofu, bananas, salt and vanilla to the blender. Process until smooth.
4. Share the banana filling between the cookie bases.
5. To make the topping, melt the chocolate chips in the microwave (it takes about a minute in mine) and stir in the coconut milk and vanilla. Divide among the banana puddings. You can either completely cover the top with chocolate or put a blob in the middle and make pretty patterns with a toothpick.
6. Place in the freezer and leave for a few hours until completely set. Serve with sliced bananas.

Chocolate Puddings with Strawberry Sauce

I don't often eat desserts, but when I do it has to be rich, fruity and chocolaty. If you want the chocolate but not the fruit, omit the strawberry sauce and make double the filling for a total chocolate-overload experience. Make sure your biscuits / cookies are vegan.

Base:
14 digestive biscuits, crushed in a plastic bag with a rolling pin (about 2 cups)
½ cup vegan margarine, melted

Sauce:
3 cups fresh strawberries
1 tsp lemon juice
½ cup organic maple syrup or raw sugar
1 tbsp corn starch

Filling:
2 avocados, pitted and scooped out
½ cup non-dairy milk
½ cup organic maple syrup
1 tbsp smooth peanut or other nut butter
1 tbsp corn starch
Pinch of salt
1 tsp pure vanilla extract
¼ cup cocoa powder
1 cup dairy free chocolate chips, melted

Makes 8 mini desserts

1. Mix the crushed cookies with the melted margarine and press into the bottom of 8 jumbo muffin cups.
2. Put the avocado, "milk", maple syrup, peanut butter, corn starch, salt, vanilla and cocoa into a blender. Process until smooth then add the melted chocolate chips and blend again.
3. Share the filling among the bases, cover with plastic wrap and pop in the fridge for a couple of hours, or, if you like frozen desserts, in the freezer.
4. Slice the strawberries and put them in a medium pan with the lemon juice, maple syrup and corn starch. Stir constantly and bring the mixture to a boil over a medium heat, then allow to cool.
5. When the puddings are completely set, carefully transfer to individual plates. If they are coming out of the freezer you should leave them at room temperature for 10 minutes before serving with the strawberry sauce.

If you have a silicone muffin or cup cake tray it will make your life a lot easier when it comes to removing the puddings. I find them much better than traditional metal ones.

Chocolate Cupcakes

It's really nice to lick uncooked cupcake batter off the spoon without worrying about getting salmonella from raw eggs. When they're cooked and cooled, top them with the icing of your choice - the ones included here are all vegan.

1 cup flour
½ tsp baking soda
¼ tsp salt
¼ cup cocoa powder
¾ cup sugar
6 tbsp vegan margarine, room temperature
1 tsp pure vanilla essence
¼ cup silken tofu, mashed
½ cup soy milk

Makes 8 - 10 standard cupcakes

1. Heat the oven to 350'F / 180'C / Gas Mark 4.
2. Lightly grease a cupcake pan or line with paper cases.
3. Mix together the flour, baking soda, salt and cocoa.
4. In a second bowl, cream together the sugar and margarine, then mix in the vanilla and mashed tofu. Beat well. Stir in the flour mixture and soy milk. Mix well.
5. Spoon the mixture into the cupcake tray and bake for 20 - 25 minutes or until a toothpick inserted in the middle comes out clean.
6. Allow to cool before topping with icing.

If you like banana chocolate cupcakes, replace the tofu with a mashed small, ripe banana

Vanilla Frosting

1 cup dairy-free margarine, soft but not melted
2½ cups powdered sugar, sifted
1 tsp vanilla extract

1. Beat the margarine and sugar together until light and fluffy, then beat in the vanilla extract.

Chocolate Icing

1 cup dairy-free margarine, soft but not melted
2½ cups powdered sugar, sifted
1 tsp vanilla extract
4 tbsp cocoa powder (sifted to get the lumps out)
3 tbsp soy milk

1. Beat the margarine and sugar together until light and fluffy, then beat in the vanilla extract.
2. Add the cocoa and soy milk. Beat it all together until creamy.

Peanut Butter Icing

5 tbsp dairy-free margarine, soft but not melted
1 cup powdered sugar, sifted
1 cup smooth peanut butter
¾ tsp vanilla extract
⅓ cup soy milk

1. Beat the margarine and sugar together until light and fluffy, then beat in the peanut butter and vanilla extract.
2. Add the soy milk and beat it all together to make a smooth icing.

Coffee Icing

½ cup dairy-free margarine, soft but not melted
3 cups powdered sugar, sifted
¼ cup strong brewed coffee, room temperature

1. Beat the margarine and sugar together until light and fluffy.
2. Gradually add the coffee and beat it all together until creamy.

Fruit Salad with "Cream"

What could be better to finish a meal than a bowl of fruit with a creamy topping? There are a number of vegan options to replace whipped cream, but this is one of my favourites.

Fruit Salad

4 - 6 cups fresh diced fruit and berries mixed with 2 tbsp unrefined raw sugar
Leave for 1 hour in the fridge for the flavours to mingle.

Hemp Milk "Whipped Cream"

I like to use hemp milk to make this cream. It has a slightly nutty aftertaste which I prefer over other non-dairy milk, but you can use soy, almond or another non-dairy milk if you prefer. Unsweetened is best since you will be adding sugar.

½ cup hemp milk
4 tbsp powdered sugar
½ tsp pure vanilla extract
1 tsp corn starch
¼ cup vegetable oil

Makes about ¾ cup

1. Put the milk, sugar, vanilla and corn starch in a blender and mix well. Add the oil and blend again until smooth and creamy. Chill for 1 hour before serving.

Want it richer? Use ¼ cup hemp milk and ½ cup oil. Want it thicker? Add an extra tablespoon of corn starch. Don't like hemp milk? Use soy or almond milk instead.

Coconut Cream

Oh my goodness - this is SO good. You can serve it with sliced fruit, dolloped on a fruit salad, or on top of shortcake or cookies.

To get coconut cream, partially open the **bottom** of an **unshaken** chilled can of premium, **high fat** coconut milk and allow the liquid to drain out. Open the can completely and there it is: coconut cream.

You will get more coconut cream from a can of premium (high fat) coconut milk than from a regular can. I like to use Rooster brand premium coconut milk for desserts, which has around 12 g of fat per 60 ml, but obviously you can use whatever is available in your local store. Indian grocery stores often have a good line of coconut milk, but read the labels to see which have a good fat content.

1 cup coconut cream
4 tbsp powdered sugar

Makes about 1 cup

1. Put the coconut cream in a small bowl and fold in the powdered sugar. Add more sugar to taste.
2. If not serving immediately, put in a covered bowl in the fridge and stir before using.

Fruit Kebabs with Chocolate Pudding

Fruit kebabs are fun to eat, and they're even better when you dip the pieces into chocolate pudding.

Fruit Kebabs

4 - 6 cups of diced fresh fruit
Wooden or metal skewers (careful - the metal edges can be sharp!)
Slide the fruit onto the wood skewers, alternating the varieties to make it look interesting.

Chocolate Pudding

2 cups soft tofu
½ cup vegetable oil
1 cup powdered sugar
¾ cup cocoa powder
½ tsp salt
4 tsp pure vanilla extract
2 tbsp corn starch

Makes about 4 half-cup servings

1. Put the tofu, oil, sugar, cocoa, salt, vanilla and corn starch in a blender and process until smooth and creamy.
2. Put in a covered bowl in the fridge for 1 hour before serving.

If you're feeling ambitious, soak your wood skewers in water for a couple of hours (or use metal skewers) and cook your kebabs on the BBQ for 5 - 10 minutes over a direct heat until softened and slightly golden in places.

Chocolate Coconut Fudge Pudding

This thick, creamy pudding is great for spreading on sliced apples, pretzels or small squares of cake.

To get coconut cream, partially open the **bottom** of an **unshaken chilled** can of **high fat / premium** coconut milk and allow the liquid to drain out. Open the can completely and there it is.

1 cup coconut cream
1 cup dairy-free dark chocolate chips
4 tbsp powdered sugar (optional)
2 tbsp water

Makes about 4 half-cup servings

1. Melt the chocolate in the microwave - it takes about 1 minute in mine - and stir well.
2. Put the coconut cream, water and sugar in a blender and pour in the melted chocolate. Blend until smooth and creamy.
3. Put in a covered bowl in the fridge for at least 1 hour before serving.

This pudding can also be made by replacing the coconut cream with soft tofu and adding 1 tbsp of vegetable oil instead of the water.

Pumpkin Pie with a Pecan Base

This sounds like a tongue twister or the beginnings of a song, but it's actually a tasty little dessert. Don't wait for thanksgiving to make it! If you have a nut allergy (or are feeling lazy) replace the nut base with a ready-made frozen pie shell from the freezer section of your local grocery store, but check the list of ingredients before you buy it.

Pecan or Walnut Base:
2 ½ cups finely chopped pecans or walnuts
¼ tsp salt
2 tbsp vegan margarine, melted

Filling:
¾ cup unrefined raw sugar
½ tsp salt
1 tsp ground cinnamon
½ tsp ground ginger
¼ tsp ground cloves
2 cups pureed pumpkin
1 cup plain non-dairy milk
¼ cup corn starch mixed with 3 tbsp water

Serves 4 -6

1. Heat the oven to 350'F / 180'C / Gas Mark 4
2. Mix together the nuts, salt and margarine. Press into a 9" round pie dish and bake for 15 minutes.
3. Turn the oven up to 425'F / 220'C / Gas Mark 7
4. Mix together the sugar, salt, cinnamon, ginger and cloves.
5. In a medium pan, mix together the pumpkin and non-dairy milk. Stir in the spices and corn starch mixture.
6. Stirring constantly, bring to the boil and allow it to thicken slightly.
7. Fill the pie crust with spiced pumpkin. Bake for 15 minutes then turn the heat down to 325'F / 170'C / Gas Mark 3 and let it cook for another 40 to 50 minutes.
7. Stick a toothpick in the pie; if it comes out clean, the pie is done. If the toothpick is sticky, cook the pie longer. It may take up to an extra 30 minutes.
8. Allow to cool for 10 minutes before serving, or allow to cool completely and serve chilled.

Pumpkin pie goes nicely with vegan vanilla ice cream. Look for ones made with soy or coconut milk.

141

Shortbread Hearts

Mmmmmmm... cookies. These are very easy to make and are really nice eaten alone or topped with coconut cream. Make sure you chill the dough before trying to roll it, and let it warm up a little after you take it out of the fridge. If it sticks to your rolling pin and countertop, sprinkle it with flour.

1 cup vegan margarine, room temperature
½ cup powdered sugar, sifted, or unrefined raw sugar
1 tsp pure vanilla extract
2 cups flour
2 ½ tsp baking powder
½ tsp salt
2 cups dairy-free chocolate chips for dipping (optional)
1 cup unsalted macadamia nuts, finely chopped (optional)
½ cup powdered sugar for coating (optional)

Makes about 25 cookies

1. Heat the oven to 350'F / 180'C / Gas Mark 4
2. In a large bowl, beat the margarine and sugar together until creamy, then add the vanilla.
3. Sift the flour, baking powder and salt together then add to the margarine mixture. Stir in the nuts (if using) then cover and chill for 1 hour.
4. On a floured surface, roll out the dough until about ¼" thick (just over ½ cm). Using a heart shaped cookie cutter or the top of a small wineglass, cut the dough into shapes. Place on a non-stick baking sheet.
5. Bake for 15 minutes or until lightly browned. Leave on the baking tray until cool then either dip in melted chocolate or cover the tops with powdered sugar shaken through a sieve.

The wholesome looking heart cookies were made using all purpose gluten-free flour (Red Mills, on this occasion) and unrefined raw sugar. The round cookies were made using organic unbleached wheat flour, powdered white sugar and macadamia nuts. Both are totally yummy.

Strawberry Shortcakes with Fruit Syrup

Does anything say "summer" quite like a strawberry shortcake? This fabulous vegan dessert can be prepared in advance and assembled just before serving. Try using different summer fruits such as peeled peaches or fresh raspberries for a bit of a change.

Strawberries:

About 3 cups washed fresh strawberries, hulled and cut into halves
2 tbsp unrefined raw sugar, plus more for sprinkling

1. Toss the strawberries with the sugar and chill until needed.

Shortcakes:

½ cup unrefined raw sugar plus an extra 2 tbsp for sprinkling
4 cups flour
5 tsp baking powder
½ tsp salt
¾ cup vegan margarine, room temperature
1 cup unsweetened plain non-dairy milk

Makes 8 shortcakes

1. Heat the oven to 400'F / 200'C / Gas Mark 6
2. Put the sugar, flour, baking powder and salt in a medium bowl and mix together.
3. Add the margarine and use your fingers to rub the margarine into the flour. It should resemble fine breadcrumbs.
4. Stir in the milk, adding a drop more milk or a bit more flour if needed, to create a firm dough.
5. Turn the dough out onto a work surface and pat into a circle about ¾" thick. Cut into about 8 - 10 circles using the top edge of a wine glass.
6. Put the shortcakes onto a baking sheet and sprinkle with the remaining sugar. Bake for 15 - 20 minutes or until golden brown. Allow to cool completely before transferring to a serving plate.

Mango Syrup:

1 large mango, finely chopped or pureed
¼ cup water
2 tbsp unrefined raw sugar
1 tsp lime juice

Makes about ½ cup

Strawberry Syrup:

2 cups strawberries, finely chopped or pureed
¼ cup water
2 tbsp unrefined raw sugar
1 tsp lime juice

1. Place the mango or strawberry puree, water and sugar in a small saucepan and warm over a medium heat, stirring until the sugar is dissolved.
2. Stir in the lime juice and serve warm.

Vanilla Coconut Cream:

1 14-ounce can / 2 cups full fat coconut milk, *chilled*.
¼ - ½ cup powdered sugar, or to taste
½ - 1 tsp pure vanilla extract, or to taste

1. Partially open the **bottom** of an **unshaken** can of chilled coconut milk and allow the liquid to drain out. Open the can completely and remove the coconut cream.
2. Add the powdered sugar and vanilla, then whip for a few minutes. Don't put it in a blender - it will separate out. Chill until needed.

Simple Coconut Cream

Follow the instructions for vanilla coconut cream, but simply fold **4 tbsp powdered sugar** into **1 cup of coconut cream**.

You can use vegan ice cream, which is becoming readily available at most grocery stores, instead of coconut cream. I prefer the ones made with coconut rather than soy.

Conversion Table

The measurements given here are rounded up or down. To make your life easier, I suggest you pop out and buy a measuring cup and some measuring spoons.

White Flour	1 cup	140g	5 oz	
Whole Wheat Flour	1 cup	130g	4 1/2 oz	
White Sugar	1 cup	225g	8 oz	
Brown Sugar (Packed)	1 cup	225g	8 oz	
Powdered Sugar	1 cup	140g	5 oz	
Chocolate Chips	1 cup	160g	6 oz	
Cocoa	1/2 cup	55g	2 oz	
Oats	1 cup	85g	3 oz	
Peanut Butter	1/2 cup	125g	4 1/2 oz	
	1 tbsp	15g	1/2 oz	
Red Lentils	1 cup	200g	7 oz	
Margarine	1 cup	225g	8 oz	
	1/2 cup	115g	4 oz	
	1 tbsp	15g	1/2 oz	
Water/ Stock/Milk	1 cup	225ml	8 oz	1/2 pint
	1/2cup	120ml	4 oz	1/4 pint
	1/4 cup	60ml	2 oz	1/8 pint
	1 tbsp	15ml	1/2 oz	
	1 tsp	5ml	1/6 oz	
Maple Syrup	1/2 cup	170g	6 oz	

Index

Vegetable Main Dishes

Salads

Hot Side Dishes

Vegan Barbeques

Sweet Treats

If you've enjoyed reading this book, check out my website at

www.helptheresavegan.com

My blog can be found at

https://helptheresavegan.wordpress.com

Lightning Source UK Ltd.
Milton Keynes UK
UKOW07f1927230915

258997UK00012B/63/P

9 780992 082604